Raymond

The

JETHRO TULL

www.pocketessentials.com

First published in Great Britain 2002 by Pocket Essentials, 18 Coleswood Road, Harpenden, Herts, AL5 1EQ

Distributed in the USA by Trafalgar Square Publishing, PO Box 257, Howe Hill Road, North Pomfret, Vermont 05053

A CIP catalogue record for this book is available from the British Library.

ISBN 1-904048-18-8

2 4 6 8 10 9 7 5 3 1

Book typeset by Wordsmith Solutions Ltd
Printed and bound by Cox & Wyman

Acknowledgements

The author thanks Ian Anderson for his help in the preparation of this book.

Sources used in the writing of this book were conversations and correspondence with Ian Anderson; *Jethro Tull—A History Of The Band, 1968-2001* by Scott Allen Nollen (McFarland & Company, Inc., 2001); *Flying Colours—The Jethro Tull Reference Manual* by Greg Russo (Crossfire Publications, 1999); the official Jethro Tull website (www.j-tull.com); *A New Day*, the Jethro Tull fan magazine (published by David Rees); and the complete catalogue of Jethro Tull albums and videos.

CONTENTS

Rating System And Author's Note

Throughout the book, the author rates Jethro Tull's albums using the criteria below. Of course, any ten Jethro Tull fans will have ten different opinions!

5/5: Excellent! Brilliant! A classic! A must-have not only for Tull fans but also for any serious rock enthusiast!

4/5: Great! Among the best of Jethro Tull's albums. Any serious Tull fan should own this one.

3/5: Very good! While not as consistently fantastic as a 4 or 5 rated entry, the more than casual fan should own it.

2/5: Fair to good, but simply not up to snuff in comparison with the stronger works. Some nice tracks mixed with some dodgy ones.

1/5: Just okay. A weaker effort but there's no such thing as a 'bad' Jethro Tull album! For the Tull completist only.

Jethro Tull compilation albums, i.e. 'best of' collections, are treated briefly and separately in chapter 7. If a compilation album contains a significant amount of unreleased material (such as *Living In The Past*), then it is included chronologically in the main text and thoroughly discussed.

Introduction:
Let Me Bring You Songs From The Wood...

How many rock bands from the 60s can you name that are still around today? Probably not many. There are a few—the Rolling Stones, Santana, Yes...—but most have broken up, stopped recording and reappear only for the ubiquitous 'reunion' tours.

Jethro Tull formed in 1968 and is still going strong, thanks to the leadership, vision and extraordinary talent of its leader Ian Anderson (who is often mistakenly identified by the ignorant and uninformed as a man named 'Jethro Tull'). Jethro Tull is the name of the *band*, not the moniker of the dynamic frontman; but it's actually not terribly surprising why this confusion occurs. Ian Anderson, for all intents and purposes, really *is* Jethro Tull. It's his band, his lyrics, his music and his personality that drive the machine. One might say that Jethro Tull is made up of Ian Anderson and whoever happens to be playing with him but this is not exactly true. One other musician is essential to the mix and that is lead guitarist Martin Barre. Without the combination of these two men, Jethro Tull would not exist. In fact, Ian Anderson has recorded solo albums and toured with a variety of musicians under his own name. It's only when Martin Barre joins him that we have Jethro Tull. While the other members of the band are certainly important and many have made names for themselves in their own right, they are for the most part expendable. After all, Anderson and Barre have been the two constants in the group for 34 years.

Jethro Tull, which celebrates its 35th anniversary in 2003, has always been controversial, challenging and completely impossible to categorise. Are they rock? Are they blues? Are they 'progressive'? Are they English folk? These labels merely begin to describe Tull's eclectic and imaginative music. In the three and a half decades of the band's life, Tull's music has gone through many styles and periods, just as the group has experienced numerous personnel changes. Nevertheless, the band has always produced distinctive 'Tull Music.' No other band plays hard rock with mandolins and flutes. No other voice sounds like Ian Anderson's—one that conjures up images of soothsayers and travelling minstrels of yore. The Jethro Tull sound is totally unique and rarely imitated and that in itself is a rarity in pop music.

Another factor that distinguishes Jethro Tull from many of today's acts is that Ian Anderson has consistently gone his own way without regard for critics, industry awards and popular trends. During the punk and new wave eras of rock music, the music press deemed that Jethro Tull was 'old fashioned' or, in Anderson's own words, "too old to rock 'n' roll." Anderson thumbed his nose at the press then and he continues to do so today, forging ahead with the steadfast intention of expressing himself the way he sees fit and of pleasing his long-time, loyal fans. He cares not a whit that the Rock and Roll Hall of Fame conveniently ignores Jethro Tull year after year. When the band won the controversial 'Best Hard Rock/Heavy Metal' Grammy Award in 1987 he was just as surprised as the audience present at the event.

In the early to mid-70s, Jethro Tull was one of the most popular bands in the world and had the clout to fill arena-sized venues. Even though the 'supergroup' status may no longer apply, Tull can still easily pack respectably large concert halls and theatres, selling out show after show all over the globe. Nearly all of their 30+ albums have gone gold and many platinum. Tull has had its share of commercial success but it's not the sole motivation that keeps Anderson and company together. Jethro Tull has endured because Anderson loves it. His dedication and passion comes through with every verse, with every strum of the guitar and with every note from that unmistakable signature flute.

The Real Jethro Tull

Believe it or not, there really was a bloke named Jethro Tull. He was an agricultural pioneer born in England in 1674. Jethro Tull originally set out to become a lawyer but instead spent several years on the Continent studying soil, culture, vegetable growing, plowing, planting and reaping. He abandoned the bar and became a full-fledged farmer. His biggest claim to fame was to invent a machine that could plant seeds in rows with any desired spacing. Thus, in 1701, a device known as the seed drill came into existence. It was horse-drawn and had three blades that cut spaced rows for seeds in the soil. Funnels behind the blades directed seeds from a seed box mounted on the drill. Tull's invention proved to be a huge success and he eventually documented his farming techniques in a book entitled *The Horse-Hoeing Husbandry, Or An Essay On The Principles Of Tillage And Vegetation...Vineyard Culture Into The Cornfields* (first published in 1731).

Coincidentally, the 17th Century Jethro Tull was also a musician. In his spare time he played the organ and purportedly mastered the instrument.

A Jethro Tull Overview

What do we think of when we hear the name Jethro Tull? What *is* 'Tull Music?' Casual fans might immediately think of songs such as 'Living In The Past,' 'Teacher,' 'Aqualung,' 'Cross-Eyed Mary,' 'Locomotive Breath,' or 'Bungle In The Jungle.' It's a fact that these songs are probably the most popular, in America anyway, and are often heard on FM radio 'classic rock' stations.

Some people might have a fondness for a very early Jethro Tull that specialised in the type of British blues pioneered by the original Fleetwood Mac and John Mayall. Those who do remember this period are probably old enough to be grandparents. It was a short-lived incarnation, lasting less than twelve months and represented by one album.

Then came the interval of what could be described as 'poetic rock.' Through a collection of clever, humorous and engaging songs, Jethro Tull found its voice and began to amass a following of considerable potency. They became stars in the UK, found critical approval, toured non-stop and recorded prolifically.

The era of concept albums and the heyday of Progressive Rock followed. This is when Jethro Tull found its American audience and earned the superstatus label, produced number one albums, played concerts in arenas and introduced opening acts such as Yes, Gentle Giant and Renaissance. Their stage shows became legendary for being innovative. Spectacular and theatrical, they incorporated costumes, sets, props, imaginative lighting effects and multimedia add-ons. Unfortunately, the music critics curiously never warmed up to Progressive Rock and thus Jethro Tull fell out of favour with the press. The legion of fans, however, grew even larger.

When musical tastes and fashions changed in the second half of the 70s, Jethro Tull's sound developed into a style that encompassed English folk and rock. It thematically embraced country life, no doubt influenced by Ian Anderson purchasing salmon farms and investing in his home country of Scotland. Again, wit and an infectious self-awareness were key ingredients to the music. There are fans that insist that this was Jethro Tull's best period.

The 80s brought changes in direction as Jethro Tull experimented with technology by bringing in synthesisers, drum machines and paring down the act to focus on the songs rather than the theatricality. Tull continued to successfully please their sizeable following of fans but had sadly lost the attention of the mainstream. This trend shifted in 1987, when Jethro Tull won the 'Hard Rock/Heavy Metal' Grammy Award, beating such acts as Metallica and AC/DC. Suddenly, Jethro Tull was fashionable again and the band was perceived to be 'grand old masters' of classic rock.

As Tull celebrated 25th and 30th anniversaries, the band gained a reputation of being one of the most successful touring outfits working in the 90s. Tull always seemed to be on the road, playing to full houses on six continents. While today some might think of them as a 'nostalgia' band, this label couldn't be further from the truth. One only has to examine the demographics of Tull's audiences. People of all ages attend the concerts, from ageing hippies to young teenagers. Tull attracts bikers, classical music enthusiasts, yuppies, housewives and head bangers. As new music continually pours out of the band, new fans are recruited. Every year a fresh generation discovers the unique and special music of Jethro Tull.

Today, Jethro Tull encompasses all of the various styles and eras the band has gone through. In an interview for the band's 25th anniversary video, Ian Anderson stated that the current incarnation had a really tough time trying to live up to all of the stylistic variances associated with Jethro Tull. Anderson is not the same guy that he was in 1968, but he is aware that he must live up to certain expectations when the band steps on stage. Many songs have been rearranged for today's audience, simply because the current band could never recapture the musical style of, say, the 1972 touring outfit. What's important is that it doesn't matter. A commonality exists through all of the various Tull line-ups: the combination of flute, electric and acoustic guitars and the unmistakable voice and wit of Ian Anderson.

Ian Anderson, The Impressionist

When asked how a song is developed from his original idea to a full-fledged recording, Ian Anderson stated: "I really wish there were a standard process—sort of a factory assembly line process—in which a song idea could go in one end, be arranged and developed, go through quality

assurance and pop out packaged and ready to be delivered to t̶
However, that is not the reality. I suppose I try to vary it w̶
song; I like to make the process different each time. The type
and subject matter dictates what that process will be. Sometimes ̶̶̶ght
be strumming the guitar and I'll come up with a phrase and a line of
lyric comes to mind. When I'm comfortable with the basic structure of a
song, I'll present it to one or two guys in the band, maybe all of them
and we work it out together. Other times I'll be playing the flute and a
melody comes into my head and the song is born that way. Recently I
was strolling through the Berlin zoo and a piece of song formed in my
head. I spent a little over an hour there and as I was leaving I had an
entire song completed!

"The lyrics don't always come first. Usually they come later; sometimes they arrive at the same time as the music. Very often the title
comes first. An idea for a title might arise and that's the inspiration for
the song. That was the case with *Too Old To Rock 'N' Roll—Too Young
To Die*. The title came first and I thought it would make a good song. I
suppose I would describe myself as a painter, but not of emotions. I'm
not a painter of abstracts or expressionistic works—although a bit of my
work ventures into that territory. I'm more of a painter of people and
landscapes. I'm an impressionist, you might say. Sometimes it's just
landscapes without the people. I'm an observer and I write about what I
see."

Anderson's impressionistic approach to songwriting is easily dis-
cernible. He writes about eccentric city characters, the foibles of school-
ing and organised religion, the plight of the farmer, the dangers of
conformity and other topics that have interested him in his travels
around the world. Added to this observational stance, Anderson brings
in an eclectic array of musical motifs from around the world. There is a
little American rhythm and blues mixed with English folk and classical
music, a touch of Indian or African sensibility and perhaps a blend of
some Russian or Eastern European ethnicity. One hesitates to place a
'World Music' label on Jethro Tull's music but that is what it is. While
much of Anderson's work is rooted in solid British ground, Jethro Tull
embraces the entire world, borrows elements from it, commingles those
components and then presents totally singular results.

There is no other band quite like Jethro Tull.

1: The Early Years (1947 – 1967)

The genius behind Jethro Tull is that fellow who often stands on one leg and plays the flute. He was once described by the press as 'a mad-dog Fagin,' was known for wearing a codpiece throughout a tour or two and was once very hirsute but isn't now.

Ian Scott Anderson, born 10 August 1947 in Dunfermline, Fifeshire, Scotland, moved to Edinburgh with his family when he was four years old. Much has been written about young Ian's early years and his rebellion against wearing a kilt at age eight and his aversion to attending Sunday School. His parents apparently forced religion upon him at a young age and this no doubt had an influence on some of the lyrics he would write later on. Songs like 'My God,' 'Hymn 43,' 'Wind-Up' and several others deal with what Anderson perceives as the absurdity of organised religion.

His parents apparently enjoyed the big bands and encouraged young Ian to learn to play the guitar. After attempting to do so on a toy ukulele, Ian persuaded his father to buy him a *real* guitar when he was eleven. It was around that time that the Anderson family moved to Blackpool, a seaside town in the north of England. There, the Andersons managed a boarding house and a neighbourhood grocery store. Ian enrolled in Blackpool Grammar School for Boys and had a knack for math and sciences. For a while he considered pursuing a career in those disciplines but this was not to be.

Early Bands

The year 1963 proved to be a catalyst of some sort. Anderson met fellow student Jeffrey Hammond (born 30 July 1946) and immediately found that they shared an interest in music. Hammond was all for starting a band. Since Ian was keen to play the guitar, Hammond picked up a bass. They soon found a drummer in the guise of another schoolmate, John Evans (born 28 March 1948). Not only could Evans play the drums, he was a fine pianist as well. Legend has it that it was Evans who introduced The Beatles' music to Anderson.

The three boys rehearsed in John's garage and soon dubbed themselves The Blades, named after the London club frequented by James Bond in Ian Fleming's popular spy novels. Anderson naturally fell into the role of lead singer and The Blades soon found themselves playing their first gig at The Holy Family youth club. Before long, they were performing weekly in churches and other youth clubs and attracting the attention of young females—which was more of a priority at the time than making any money.

After a while, Michael Stephens, a guitarist from a rival band called The Atlantics, joined The Blades. In 1964, the band advertised in the local paper for a drummer because Evans preferred playing keyboards and kept hurting his hands on the drum kit. Barrie Barlow (born 10 September 1949) answered the call. Experienced as a school band drummer, Barlow got the job and Evans purchased a portable organ. Throughout the rest of the year, The Blades built a local reputation playing pop and blues songs that they had learned by listening to records.

When Ian Anderson graduated from Blackpool Grammar he felt a responsibility to get a 'proper' job. He worked in a department store for a while and then he applied to be a policeman. Luckily, he was turned away for being only sixteen. Instead, Anderson did something sensible and enrolled in the Blackpool College of Art to study painting. He never amounted to much as a painter because his musical endeavours received more of his attention.

Things really started cooking in 1965. The Blades added Jim Doolin on trumpet and baritone sax and Martin Skyrme on tenor sax, adding an entirely new dynamic to the band's sound. Michael Stephens left and it was decided that the group needed a new name. Jeffrey Hammond suggested that John Evans drop the 's' at the end of his name because it sounded better. This led to the metamorphosis into The John Evan Band. They were billed as the John Evan Blues Band at their first gig in December at the Blackpool Grammar School for Boys. By 1966, another Atlantics alumnus, Chris Riley, joined as guitarist. The John Evan Band even acquired a manager, an electrician named Johnny Taylor. More lucrative gigs came about after a two-day talent competition at the Elizabethan Club in Kirkam in March 1966.

Their repertoire now consisted of covering material by the Graham Bond Organisation, Sonny Terry and Brownie McGhee, John Lee Hooker and James Brown. But this changed, just as music itself was changing in 1966. The John Evan Band line-up was also mercurial but the core members of Anderson, Hammond, Evans, Barlow and Riley stuck it out. Eventually the band was playing higher-profile gigs at universities and larger clubs like the Bolton Palais. Perhaps their biggest claims to fame at the time were opening for Herman's Hermits in June 1966 at the British Cellophone and '99' clubs in Barrow and then sharing the bill with Graham Bond and John Mayall's Bluesbreakers (with Eric Clapton!) at various boat clubs.

It was a tough life. John Evans was the only member who had a driver's licence and owned a van. For every gig, the lads would load, travel, unload, rehearse, perform, reload, travel and unload again—night after night. The money was poor and morale was low. Despite the hard life, the band surprisingly continued to get work. The obvious next step was to make some demos. Using crude equipment in Evans' garage, the band recorded Thelonius Monk's 'Straight, No Chaser' and the first known Ian Anderson composition—'How Can You Work With Mama.'

Jeffrey Hammond eventually threw in the towel and enrolled in the Blackpool College of Art to become a painter full time. Chris Riley and Barrie Barlow became casualties soon after. Replacements included Derek 'Bo' Ward, Neil Smith and Ritchie Dharma. The band also changed managers, even though it appeared that the group would completely fall apart. But Anderson was intent on pursuing a career in music. After two years, he dropped out of art school and took up more odd jobs to make pocket money.

Neil Smith recorded a date that the band played in October 1966 in Casterton so that he could practise at home while listening to the tape. In 1989, Smith unearthed the tape and gave it to David Rees, editor and publisher of a Jethro Tull fanzine called *A New Day*. Ian Anderson gave Rees permission to release the album, warts and all, as *The John Evan Band—Live '66*. Sold in 1990 as a limited edition through *A New Day* in both cassette and CD formats, this bootleg-quality trinket represents the earliest available recording of Ian Anderson and company in performance.

The group became The John Evan Smash when they opened for Pink Floyd at the Canterbury Technical College in Kent in late 1966. Apparently the new manager, Don Read, thought this name better suited the times.

In early 1967, more personnel changes occurred. Barrie Barlow, after hearing and being very impressed with the John Evan Smash, wanted back in. He brought along a new bass player, Blackpool resident Glenn Cornick (born 23 April 1947 as Glenn Douglas Barnard, but he adopted his stepfather's surname). The line-up now consisted of Anderson,

14

Evans, Barlow, Cornick, Neil Smith, Tony Wilkinson and Neil Valentine. This assortment proved to be the best yet. The group specialised in a type of north England soul music that was very popular in those parts. Anderson's songwriting skills continued to blossom, albeit slowly. The band performed another original composition, 'Take The Easy Way,' on a television talent program called *Firstimers*. It was broadcast on 24 May 1967, but the band didn't win the contest and unfortunately the tape of the show no longer exists. Not to be discouraged, the band promptly went into Regent Sound Studio in London in late May/early June to lay down Anderson's two compositions. Today these recordings are considered lost because they only exist on poor acetates and tape reels.

London was the place to be if one wanted to break into the big time. The band desperately needed a manager who could book them there. This line of thinking meant that Don Read was out and a Manchester-based concert booker named Chris Wright was in. Wright and his partner Terry Ellis had their own booking agency in London and managed Ten Years After. The John Evan Smash signed on with Ellis/Wright and by the end of the summer had more dates in the big city.

This led to the band's first official recording session for producer Derek Lawrence. Lawrence wanted to call the band Candy Coloured Rain. The boys hated that, but they were willing to put up with it for the opportunity to lay down demos at EMI studios in London. Four new Ian Anderson compositions were recorded along with a couple of covers but EMI ultimately destroyed the tapes because they 'took up space.'

The Business Of Flutes,
Mick Abrahams And Moving South

Ian Anderson acquired his first flute because of a debt. Someone owed him some money and when he and Glenn Cornick showed up to collect, all the person had in hand was a Selmer Gold Seal concert flute in C. Anderson accepted the instrument as payment. He didn't know how to play it so he taught himself. Never mind that he held it wrong, blew it improperly and his technique probably would have given nightmares to a classically trained flautist. Anderson's inspiration grew after hearing Roland Kirk's LP *I Talk With The Spirits*, a jazz album that featured an abundance of flute. Kirk's song 'Serenade To A Cuckoo' became the first tune that Anderson learned to play on his new-found instrument, adding it to his range of abilities that included composing, vocals, guitar, drums and harmonica. Little did he know that the flute would become his signature instrument.

The John Evan Smash went into EMI's Abbey Road studio in October 1967 to record once again under the supervision of Derek Lawrence. The sessions produced a new song penned by Anderson and Cornick (credited to Anderson/Barnard, Cornick's real name) called 'Aeroplane.' One of Lawrence's protégés, Tony Wilson, sang backup on the song and later gained fame with the pop band Hot Chocolate. The other song was Anderson's alone, entitled 'Letting You Go' and featured his new flute for the first time. Both tunes would go unreleased for the time being.

The planets must have been in alignment on 27 October 1967, when the John Evan Smash played a gig in Luton, near London, at the Beachcomber Discotheque. Sharing the stage was a band called McGregor's Engine, which featured guitarist Mick Abrahams, drummer Clive Bunker and bassist Andy Pyle. Abrahams (born 7 April 1943) was impressed with the on-stage antics of the twenty-year-old singer and flute player. Anderson was mutually awed by Abrahams' guitar ability, which gravitated toward blues and R&B. One thing led to another and Anderson invited Abrahams to join the band. The only problem was that Abrahams lived in Luton and had no desire to move to Blackpool, or even London for that matter. When the Smash got back to Blackpool, morale was at an all time low, every member was in some kind of financial debt and the pressure of finding 'real' jobs was immense. Neil Smith left, which opened up the guitar slot for Abrahams. There was only one thing to do—move south.

Once the band got to Luton and the London area, everyone was broke. Chris Wright managed to get the band a few gigs featuring the new guitarist, but the John Evan Smash fell apart. Barrie Barlow quit for the second time to go back home to his girlfriend in Blackpool. John Evans decided to continue his college studies and went home. Within a few weeks everyone but Anderson, Cornick and Abrahams had gone missing. To replace Barlow, Abrahams brought in Clive Bunker (born 12 December 1946) from McGregor's Engine. By November 1967, the band with no name consisted of: Anderson on vocals, flute, harmonica and occasional guitar; Abrahams on lead guitar and occasional vocals; Cornick on bass; and Bunker on drums. One of the problems at this point was that the John Evan Smash still had a few bookings left to play and the venues expected a septet. When the new band arrived at the gigs, they had to explain that the missing members were in the hospital for some reason.

Management-wise, Chris Wright was devoting more of his time to Ten Years After, so his partner Terry Ellis took the new group under his wing. Ellis continued to book the new quartet under various names, including 'Ian Anderson's Blues Band,' 'Ian Anderson's Bag O' Nails,' 'Ian *Henderson's* Bag O' Nails,' 'Bag O' Blues' and 'Navy Blue.' The old practice of frequently renaming the group so that they could get a second gig someplace under the guise of being a 'different' band paid off. But by the end of 1967 it was clear that the group needed an identity that would distinguish them from what had gone before.

2: The Birth Of Jethro Tull (1968 – 1970)

In early 1968, the quartet went about completing the demo record-ings that the John Evan Smash had begun a few months earlier. Derek Lawrence had got a contract with MGM to release a single and so the band went back to Abbey Road Studios to remix 'Aeroplane' and record a new tune, penned by Mick Abrahams, entitled 'Sunshine Day.' Tony Wilson once again sang backup vocals. Now all they needed was a name to put on the label.

Dave Robson, an agent with the Ellis/Wright agency, suggested that they use the name 'Jethro Tull,' after the inventor of the seed drill. 'It had a nice grubby farmer sound to it,' was the reasoning. When the band played their first gig at the prestigious Marquee Club on 2 Febru-ary 1968, that was the name they used. It stuck. Marquee manager John Gee liked the band enormously and was especially taken with Ian Anderson's wild performance on flute, harmonica and vocals. Gee promptly awarded Jethro Tull a Friday night residency at the club, where they performed every other week.

The MGM single was released on 16 February to take advantage of the Marquee debut. There are varying accounts as to why the error occurred, but for some strange reason, the name of the band on the sin-gle's label was printed as 'Jethro Toe!' Derek Lawrence blamed an MGM staffer as having misheard the name over the telephone, but it's also possible that Lawrence himself made the mistake because he had been heard to pronounce the group's name as such. Some say that Lawrence did it on purpose because he didn't like the name Jethro Tull.

In the long run it didn't really matter. The 'Sunshine Day'/ 'Aeroplane' single came and went without much notice. No one is exactly sure how many copies it sold, but the single is extremely rare today. An authentic copy sells for as much as $1,000! Considered long lost after many years, the two tracks were unearthed for the *20 Years Of Jethro Tull* box set that was released in 1988. Listening to them now, it's understandable why the single didn't do well. 'Sunshine Day' is a pleasant enough jazz ditty and 'Aeroplane' has a strong slow tempo that showcases Anderson's voice, but at the end of the day neither song is particularly memorable.

Since MGM made a mess of the first recording, it was decided that the Ellis/Wright agency would form their own record company to handle the acts that they managed. Thus, Chrysalis Productions was formed, the genesis of what would become Chrysalis Records.

Gigs, A Festival And The First Album

As 1968 rolled into spring, Ian Anderson took it upon himself to force his way into the role of frontman. Chrysalis attempted to push Abrahams into that spot but Anderson fiercely resisted. His songwriting skills improved and he gave the band some individualistic numbers to perform live. A tattered, long overcoat became a staple costume for Anderson and it, along with his long, dishevelled hair, gave him a rather scruffy, homeless appearance. In counterpoint to this was his on-stage banter. When he spoke it was immediately apparent that the man was intelligent and witty. Using this 'brainy tramp' persona to his advantage, Anderson developed a stage act that included standing on one leg while playing the harmonica and flute, leaping about, bulging his eyes and mugging at the audience and 'directing' the other band members with flamboyant gestures. There was no doubt that he was a charismatic performer.

Jethro Tull slowly gained a reputation as a live act. The Marquee residency certainly helped, but a June 1968 free concert in London's Hyde Park, opening for Pink Floyd, got the attention of John Peel, the influential BBC radio impresario known for promoting bands that were not particularly mainstream. In early August 1968, Jethro Tull was invited by Peel to record a session for the *Top Gear* program. Anderson had written a song for his long-time friend Jeffrey Hammond, appropriately entitled, 'A Song for Jeffrey.' This downright weird bluesy number with distorted vocals was the showcase of the session. Anderson's 'My Sunday Feeling' and a Sonny Terry and Brownie McGhee number, 'So Much Trouble,' were also recorded. The program aired on 22 September 1968.

On 10 August, Jethro Tull performed at the 8th Sunbury National Jazz & Blues Festival in Kempton, which proved to be another fortuitous event. A sold-out crowd of 20,000 attended the three-day festival and Tull appeared on the same day alongside such heavyweights as Deep Purple, Fairport Convention, John Mayall, The Spencer Davis Group, Traffic and The Incredible String Band. The audience was sufficiently wowed by Tull's performances of 'Serenade To A Cuckoo' and 'Cat's Squirrel.' The reception surprised everyone in the band, for most of the Marquee fans turned out in force to cheer them on. In the audience that day were two fellows who would soon play important parts in the Jethro Tull history book—Martin Barre and David Palmer. They, too, were impressed with Jethro Tull.

In fact, Palmer (born 2 July 1937), a professional composer, arranger and conductor, was already working with Jethro Tull. He had been brought in to arrange a horn section for the recording of Mick Abrahams' song 'Move On Alone.' This, along with 'A Song For Jeffrey,' 'Serenade To A Cuckoo' and other songs from the current stage set were being laid down for what would be the first official Jethro Tull album. Terry Ellis and Chris Wright had made a deal with Island Records to distribute Chrysalis Productions' recordings (and Reprise was secured to handle the task in the US). Recording had begun in June and continued through the summer until the album was completed.

A preview single was released on 27 September 1968 consisting of 'A Song For Jeffrey'/'One For John Gee.' The latter was an instrumental jazz number that Abrahams wrote and dedicated to the band's supporter at the Marquee Club. Finally, at the end of October, Jethro Tull's first LP was unleashed.

This Was

Released: UK: October 1968; US: February 1969

Track List: My Sunday Feeling (Anderson); Someday The Sun Won't Shine For You (Anderson); Beggar's Farm (Anderson/Abrahams); Move On Alone (Abrahams); Serenade To A Cuckoo (Roland Kirk); Dharma For One (Anderson/Bunker); It's Breaking Me Up (Anderson); Cat's Squirrel (traditional); A Song For Jeffrey (Anderson); Round (Anderson/Abrahams/Cornick/Bunker/Ellis).

Note: A 2002 CD reissue was remastered and contained the bonus tracks 'One For John Gee,' 'Love Story' and 'A Christmas Song.'

Cover Art: Conceived by Terry Ellis and Brian Ward. Photographed by Brian Ward. Jethro Tull would always be known for unusual and innovative album covers and *This Was* is no exception. The band members are pictured wearing theatrical make-up and costumes, masquerading as very old men. They are standing (Anderson is sitting) among a mixed litter of dogs and staring at the camera. The name 'Jethro Tull' is prominent (only on the US cover—the UK cover has no text on it) but one has to turn the LP over to see the true title, *This Was*. Packaged as a gatefold, the inside depicts a blurry photograph of the band on stage. The back cover shows the band sans make-up, glaring at the camera. Anderson is holding a fish skeleton and is grinning like a fool. Strange indeed.

Personnel: Ian Anderson (vocals, flute, harmonica, piano, claghorn); Mick Abrahams (electric guitar, nine-string guitar, vocals on 'Move On Alone'); Glenn Cornick (bass guitar); Clive Bunker (drums, hooter, charm bracelet). Brass arrangements: David Palmer. Produced by Terry Ellis and Jethro Tull. Recording Engineer: Victor Gamm.

Recording Background: The album is a fairly good representation of the first Tull line-up and its live repertoire. It's the only Tull album that is almost entirely blues oriented, a style that the band wouldn't return to except for occasional forays in the 90s. Ian Anderson must have had an inkling that the band wouldn't continue in this direction, hence the title of the album. As he explains in the liner notes, "This was how we were playing then… but things change. Don't they."

Comments: This Was is a mixed bag of blues and jazz numbers that doesn't entirely work as a whole. Individual numbers—'My Sunday Feeling,' 'Beggar's Farm,' 'Serenade To A Cuckoo' and 'A Song For Jeffrey' stand out, but the rest of the tracks don't quite come together. Abrahams' tour de force on guitar, 'Cat's Squirrel,' is raucous and lively but it goes on a bit too long and his own composition, the brassy 'Move On Alone,' seems particularly out of place. Through several songs, especially 'Jeffrey,' Anderson intentionally filters his voice sonically so that it sounds tinny, as if it were coming out of an antique radio. The effect is bizarre. Oddly, there is just as much harmonica on the album as there is flute. In hindsight, it is quite evident that *This Was* is an album in search of a singular voice. Long-time Tull fans have varied reactions to *This Was.* Many of them don't consider it representative of the Jethro Tull they know and indeed it is different from every subsequent Tull LP. On the other hand, blues fans love the album simply because it's raw, unpolished and features a great deal of improvisation.

Trivia: This Was sold well, hitting #10 on the UK album chart. It didn't break the top 50 in America (#62). There was some speculation that Jethro Tull performed at the Woodstock festival in 1969 because the band can be heard in the background during some of the crowd scenes in the documentary concert film released in 1970. Actually, *This Was* was being played over the sound system in between acts. It was perhaps the first time that many American audience members had heard the band!

Verdict: An enjoyable and historic album, but simply not representative of what Jethro Tull eventually became. 2/5

A New Day

Despite having the satisfaction of releasing a critically well-received album and building a loyal audience of supporters in the UK, all was not hunky-dory within the band. Ian Anderson and Mick Abrahams ultimately came to the crossroad so often cited in the histories of rock bands—artistic differences. Anderson wanted to take the band's musical direction away from the blues. He had already penned a new song that featured a mandolin, 'Love Story,' and an acoustic, quiet number called 'A Christmas Song,' both slated to appear on Tull's next single. Recorded in November, the single's A-side featured the entire band, but Ian Anderson performed 'A Christmas Song' alone. David Palmer was once again brought in to arrange strings. This in itself indicated to Mick Abrahams that he was not in charge. The single was released at the end of November.

Another sore point between the two men was that Abrahams had no desire to play more than four nights a week or leave England. The others were itching to play gigs outside of the country and, especially, tackle America when *This Was* was released there. Thus, a tense Jethro Tull continued to play their UK commitments for the rest of November but by December Anderson had had enough of Abrahams. Abrahams' feelings were mutual.

Anderson hastily put together auditions for a new guitarist because the band was scheduled to appear on *The Rolling Stones Rock & Roll Circus* television special on 10 December. One of the young men auditioning was Martin Barre, who had seen the band play at the Sunbury Festival. At the time, Anderson felt that Barre was too shy and Barre readily admitted that he didn't play particularly well. Tony Iommi, later of Black Sabbath fame, got the job but this proved to be only temporary. Iommi never felt like he fit in with the Jethro Tull dynamic so it was agreed that the television special would be his only gig with the band.

Chrysalis booked Tull to travel to America in February 1969 to promote *This Was*. The band desperately needed a guitarist. Anderson remembered Martin Barre from the auditions and called him back.

Barre (born 17 November 1946) had a good deal of experience playing with various bands but was studying architecture. Luckily, his second audition fared much better and Barre was inducted into the band. From this point on, he would be the only member besides Anderson to stay with Jethro Tull to the present day. In fact, Barre's lead guitar work became so important to Tull's overall sound that it is impossible to imagine the band without him.

Jethro Tull made an auspicious impact on their first visit to the United States. They played the Fillmore East, opening for Blood, Sweat and Tears and later supported such acts as Led Zeppelin, Fleetwood Mac and Vanilla Fudge. Chrysalis also booked them as headliners in smaller clubs and venues. While they were in the States, the band recorded a new single, 'Living In The Past,' a song that would eventually become one of Tull's signature pieces. Incorporating an infectious 5/4 time signature and a catchy melody, the song showcased Anderson's flute playing and hit-writing ability. It was released in the UK in May 1969 with 'Driving Song' on the back, and reached #3 in the charts. The US release went unnoticed but it was re-released a few years later and was a huge hit.

By then, the band was back in England, recording *Stand Up*, their second, pivotal LP. They appeared on *Top Of The Pops* in June, continued touring and went back to America for the rest of the summer. While they were there, the band learned that *Stand Up* had shot to #1 in the UK.

Stand Up

Released: UK: August 1969; US: September 1969

Track List: A New Day Yesterday; Jeffrey Goes To Leicester Square; Bourée; Back To The Family; Look Into The Sun; Nothing Is Easy; Fat Man; We Used To Know; Reasons For Waiting; For A Thousand Mothers. (All songs by Ian Anderson, except 'Bourée' by J. S. Bach.)

Note: A 2002 CD reissue was remastered and contained the bonus tracks 'Living In The Past,' 'Driving Song,' 'Sweet Dream' and '17.'

Cover Art: Conceived by Terry Ellis and John Williams, printed from woodcuts by Jimmy Grashow. This is a wonderful cover, featuring caricatures of the band in woodcuts on front and back. The gatefold opens to reveal a pop-up cut-out of all four members—they 'stand up,' so to speak.

Personnel: Ian Anderson (vocals, flute, acoustic guitar, Hammond organ, piano, mandolin, balalaika, harmonica); Martin Barre (electric guitar, flute); Glenn Cornick (bass guitar); Clive Bunker (drums and percussion). Strings arranged and conducted by David Palmer. Produced by Terry Ellis and Ian Anderson. Recording Engineer: Andy Johns.

Recording Background: As Jethro Tull departed for America in early 1969, Ian Anderson was writing songs like a madman. They were a completely different batch of tunes than what had appeared on *This Was*. Poet-songwriters such as Bob Dylan and Roy Harper were now influencing Anderson and this was reflected in the new material. More introspective and folk-driven, the songs also brought in classical elements that gave them a more progressive, modern feel. The only blues number in the bunch was 'A New Day Yesterday.'

Comments: The songs are reportedly about Ian Anderson's relationship with his parents. The simplistic nature of the album is its strength. While there are some rockers ('A New Day Yesterday,' 'Nothing Is Easy,' 'For A Thousand Mothers'), there are a couple of quiet, melodic pieces ('Look Into The Sun,' 'Reasons For Waiting') and some ethnic, Eastern-influenced ones ('Jeffrey Goes To Leicester Square,' 'Fat Man'). The album's highlight is the instrumental 'Bourée,' which became another signature piece for the band. It showcased not only Anderson's flute playing ability but also Glenn Cornick's bass guitar work. By taking Bach's baroque piece and infusing it with jazzy improvisation, Tull created a true 'classic' piece of rock. 'Jeffrey Goes To Leicester Square' is the second song written for Jeffrey Hammond and is pleasant and lively. 'Nothing Is Easy' is a superb number with a wonderful swing tempo. 'Fat Man' is a humorous song played on mandolin, balalaika, flute and Eastern percussion. The wit and intelligence behind the lyrics is immediately apparent, making it one of the very best of Jethro Tull's albums. As a testament to its greatness, many of the songs still feature in concerts today.

Trivia: 'Bourée' is mistakenly credited to Ian Anderson in the liner notes! Further recordings on other albums correctly credited J. S. Bach. Martin Barre plays the flute on 'Fat Man' and a second flute line on 'Bourée.' The album went to #1 in Britain and reached #20 in the US.

24

Verdict: Easily one of the five best albums Jethro Tull ever recorded. 5/5

Tull Conquers America

The band spent the rest of 1969 touring. A single was recorded, 'Sweet Dream' with '17' as the B-side. An out-take, 'Singing All Day,' was held back for a later date. 'Sweet Dream' is a terrific rocker with unusual syncopation and a marvellous string arrangement by David Palmer. '17,' on the other hand, even by Anderson's admission, is one of the worst Jethro Tull cuts ever recorded!

The 20 September 1969 issue of *Melody Maker* published their poll of most popular British groups and Jethro Tull was the runner-up behind The Beatles. The Rolling Stones came in third!

Around this time much was made in the press about Ian Anderson's solid anti-drug stance. He claimed to have never taken drugs and to this day he stands by the statement. Given his shabby appearance in those days, his words were naturally met with some scepticism. Nevertheless, Anderson has continually supported anti-drug causes, discouraged drug abuse by band members and has been known to chastise audience members who smoke illegal substances close to the stage.

Another single was recorded in December, this time with the help of old bandmate John Evans. He played keyboards for 'The Witch's Promise' and 'Teacher,' two very strong songs by Anderson. 'The Witch's Promise' is an elegant and whimsical piece with unusual time signatures and a lot of flute, while 'Teacher' is more of a heavy rocker with impressive Martin Barre guitar work. There are two versions of 'Teacher' floating around. The first, the one that appeared on the single, is slower and contains no flute. The second version is one better known to American audiences—it is faster, has a flute in it and appeared on the US single release.

As a result of Evans' welcome participation on the single, he was asked to play on Tull's next studio album, *Benefit*, after which he became a fully-fledged fifth member of the band. Once again, he dropped the 's' at the end of his surname and would be forever credited as 'John Evan.'

Benefit

Released: UK: May 1970; US: April 1970

Track List: With You There To Help Me; Nothing To Say; Alive And Well And Living In*; Son; For Michael Collins, Jeffrey And Me; To Cry You A Song?; A Time For Everything; Inside*; Play In Time; Sossity—You're A Woman. (All songs by Ian Anderson.)

* The UK edition is as shown. The US edition substituted 'Alive And Well And Living In' with 'Inside' on side one and the second mix of 'Teacher' for 'Inside' on side two. Thus, 'Teacher' is not on the UK edition and 'Alive And Well And Living In' is not on the US edition.

Note: A 2002 CD reissue was remastered and contained the bonus tracks 'Singing All Day,' 'The Witch's Promise,' 'Just Trying To Be' and 'Teacher.'

Cover Art: Designed by Terry Ellis and Ruan O'Lochlainn, photography by Ruan O'Lochlainn, graphic presentation by Ken Reilly. *Benefit* shows four cut-out stand-ups of the band members, as if they had been punched out of die-cut cardboard. They are standing on a stage in front of a picture window, behind which peer the faces of the band. A rectangular portal frames the entire composition.

Personnel: Ian Anderson (vocals, flute, acoustic and electric guitars); Martin Barre (acoustic and electric guitars); Glenn Cornick (bass guitar); Clive Bunker (drums, percussion); John Evan (piano, Hammond organ). Produced by Ian Anderson (Executive Producer Terry Ellis). Recording Engineer: Robin Black.

Recording Background: The songs on *Benefit* reflect Ian Anderson's disenchantment with non-stop touring. He had become more withdrawn and solitary, spending what little free time he had holed up in hotel rooms. He was also pining for his girlfriend, Jennie Franks, a secretary at Chrysalis, whom he would marry later in the year. *Benefit* is a pessimistic album and much of the wit and humour that was present in *Stand Up* is missing. Indeed, the band's touring schedule was brutal—three tours to the US in 1969, two in 1970, plus UK and European outings in between. There was almost never a moment's rest.

Comments: Despite the lack of humour on the album, *Benefit* is one of the strongest Jethro Tull albums and one that was successful in attracting more listeners in America. There is more hard rock on this album; Martin Barre drives it with powerful riffs in nearly every song. Except for two quiet, acoustic numbers ('For Michael Collins, Jeffrey

And Me' and 'Sossity—You're A Woman'), the album is fully electric (and even the quiet songs contain rocking middle-eights). The addition of John Evans on keyboards fills out the sound wonderfully. Highlights include: 'With You There To Help Me,' which has a mystical, eerie quality to it, thanks to some well-engineered reverb; 'Inside,' the most playful and whimsical tune on the album (and released as a single in the US only); 'To Cry You A Song?' and its memorable guitar groove; and 'Teacher' (on the US edition), a song that still gets FM radio airplay today. Perhaps the only problem with the LP is a lack of sonic variety, which wasn't an issue on the diverse *Stand Up*.

Trivia: Benefit was another UK hit, charting at #3. It made it to #11 in the US. 'For Michael Collins, Jeffrey And Me' is yet another song with a tip of the hat to Jeffrey Hammond; Collins is a NASA astronaut.

Verdict: This album rocks. If there had been a touch more variety in the arrangements and sonic dynamics, as was present in *Stand Up*, it would have been an unqualified classic. 4/5

3: Supergroup (1971 – 1976)

Tull continued touring through 1970, now headlining most of their shows. An appearance at the Isle of Wight Festival on 30 August was a major event, caught for prosperity on film for a feature that wouldn't be released until over twenty years later!

One of the most important gigs was a benefit concert held at Carnegie Hall in New York City. The Beatles had been the only other rock band to perform at Carnegie Hall until Jethro Tull took the stage on 4 November 1970. The charity was Phoenix House, a drug rehabilitation centre in New York. Once again, Anderson trumpeted his anti-drug stance.

The Carnegie Hall concert was recorded and parts of it filmed. Two long pieces were released on the compilation album *Living In The Past* (1972) and the remainder of the concert was released as part of the lavish *25th Anniversary Box Set* (1993). It is apparent from listening to the show that it was a corker. One of the new songs previewed on the 1970 tour was Anderson's scathing observation of organised religion, 'My God.' A *tour de force* of lyrical profundity and structurally dynamic music, the song would ultimately be thought of as one of the band's very best.

At the end of the US tour in 1970, Glenn Cornick was let go. Reportedly, Anderson fired him because he didn't condone the bass player's lifestyle. Cornick liked to party and enjoy the role of rock star, i.e. partake of drugs, alcohol and women. Anderson ran a tight ship and Cornick simply didn't fit in with the desired atmosphere.

Luckily, another John Evan Band alumnus was waiting in the wings. Jeffrey Hammond had left art school and was hanging loose when Anderson asked him if he'd like to play in a band again. Although he hadn't played the bass in years, Hammond rose to the challenge and rehearsed like a maniac for two weeks in December. Because the music had grown considerably more complex, he had a difficult time. Anderson had to teach him each song, note for note. Miraculously, Hammond was ready when the band went into the studios at the end of December to begin recording their fourth and most famous album, *Aqualung*. Anderson and Hammond decided that the new bass player would always be credited as Jeffrey Hammond-Hammond for no apparent reason other than that it sounded silly.

Aqualung

Released: UK: March 1971; US: May 1971

Track List: (The first six tracks have an overall title of 'Aqualung' and the next five tracks have an overall title of 'My God.') Aqualung: Aqualung; Cross-Eyed Mary; Cheap Day Return; Mother Goose; Wond'ring Aloud; Up To Me; My God: My God; Hymn 43; Slipstream; Locomotive Breath; Wind-Up. (All songs by Ian Anderson except for 'Aqualung' words by Jennie Anderson.)

Note: A 25th anniversary CD reissue was remastered and contained the bonus tracks 'Lick Your Fingers Clean,' 'Wind-Up' (quad version remix), 'Interview With Ian Anderson,' 'A Song For Jeffrey' (BBC *Top Gear* version), 'Fat Man' (BBC *Top Gear* version) and 'Bourée' (BBC *Top Gear* version).

Cover Art: Paintings by Burton Silverman. A painting of a homeless street tramp (which looks amazingly like Ian Anderson—wink wink) adorns the cover of Jethro Tull's most recognisable album. The lettering is a Gothic style that became identified with the band as an unofficial logo. The back cover shows the same tramp sitting on the pavement, looking forlorn. The gatefold opens to reveal another marvellous painting of the entire band frolicking in what appears to be a medieval tavern. Of note is that the texture of the original LP paper stock feels like real canvas.

Personnel: Ian Anderson (vocals, flute, acoustic and electric guitars, percussion); Martin Barre (electric guitar, descant recorder); John Evan (piano, Hammond organ, mellotron); Jeffrey Hammond-Hammond (bass guitar, alto recorder, vocals); Clive Bunker (drums, percussion). Orchestra arranged and conducted by David Palmer. Produced by Ian Anderson (Executive Producer Terry Ellis). Recording Engineer: John Burns.

Recording Background: The band went directly into the recording studio two weeks after Jeffrey Hammond joined the group. Because the songs were much more complex than what had gone before, initial group discussions and rehearsals went longer than they were accustomed to. The title song was inspired by an idea from Ian Anderson's new bride, Jennie, who had taken some photos of homeless people along the Thames River. One of these characters struck Anderson as the ideal subject for a song. Jennie wrote the words and Ian composed the music. The 'Aqualung' set of songs deals with London street life and a motley crew of misfits, such as the town prostitute, Cross-Eyed Mary. The 'My God' suite of songs came under more scrutiny from critics as it deals specifically with religion and Anderson's personal frustrations with it. There is cynicism there but Anderson also invites the listener to not take life too seriously. *Aqualung* was called a 'concept album,' although Anderson has always denied that this is so. Nevertheless, the street life theme runs through half of the album and the religious theme runs through the other half. Intentional or not, the album *is* conceptual and is a hallmark of the Progressive Rock era.

Comments: Aqualung will be the album for which Jethro Tull is remembered. It's the one that could be dropped into a time capsule, pulled out a hundred years from now and seen as representing the band. It has everything that is associated with Tull: humour; cynicism; loud hard rock; quiet, acoustic pieces; medieval and Renaissance influences; intellectual subject matter; intricate arrangements; and virtuoso musicianship. The sequencing of the album is particularly smart. Anderson breaks up the album by inserting short, acoustic numbers between the rockers so that the listener can catch his breath. The title song is and will always be a classic rock anthem, an epic poem that goes from hard, thundering rock to a haunting, melodic middle, then back to the explosive rock. Martin Barre's solo in the latter third soars to great heights. Every song is a highlight but the other standouts are the blistering 'Cross-Eyed Mary,' the playful 'Mother Goose' with its cast of fairytale characters, the poignant love song 'Wond'ring Aloud,' the cynical and powerful 'My God,' the other rock anthem on the LP 'Locomotive Breath' and Anderson's final word on religion 'Wind-Up.' Jethro Tull cannot perform a concert today without playing 'Aqualung' and/or 'Locomotive Breath.' In short, *Aqualung* is a masterpiece.

Trivia: A song called 'Lick Your Fingers Clean' was scheduled to be on the album but was dropped at the last minute. Anderson's reasoning was that it just didn't fit smoothly with the rest of the album. It was almost released as a single separately but that idea was scrapped as well. The song was reworked with some new lyrics and a new arrangement, retitled 'Two Fingers' and put on the *WarChild* album in 1974. The original song finally appeared on the *20 Years Of Jethro Tull* box set in 1988 and on the aforementioned remastered CD reissue in 1996. A quadraphonic remix of the album was also released in 1971. This contained strikingly different mixes of some of the songs, especially 'Wind-Up.' The remixed version of 'Aqualung' appeared on the

M.U.—The Best Of Jethro Tull compilation in 1975. *Aqualung* was not a number one album on first release (#4 in the UK, #7 in the US), but it has consistently sold extremely well up to the present day and is easily Tull's biggest-selling album.

Verdict: Many would say it's the quintessential Jethro Tull album. 5/5

Hitting The Top

With the success of *Aqualung*, Jethro Tull suddenly found themselves worldwide stars. The back catalogue was selling well, they were *the* act to see live and it appeared that the many years of struggling as a fledgling band in Blackpool had finally paid off. Clive Bunker, however, felt the need to depart. The band's new material really didn't suit him and he wanted to get married and live a more relaxed domestic life in England. Just after *Aqualung* was released, the call went out to yet another former John Evan Band alumnus—Barrie Barlow. Barlow had been working as a lathe turner and played occasionally with local bands when he rejoined the group. He took Bunker's place on the drum kit and, like Hammond, had some fun with his name, which became 'Barriemore' Barlow on album liner notes.

Jethro Tull was now made up of Ian Anderson, the only original member, three guys from the old John Evan Band and Martin Barre. It was a line-up that would have some longevity.

In May 1971 they recorded what would be a five-track EP entitled *Life Is A Long Song*. The title track stands as one of the great Ian Anderson songs. The lyrics are simultaneously clever and poignant and it has a strong melody. 'Up The Pool' is an affectionate remembrance of growing up in Blackpool. 'Nursie' was written for Ian's father, who had been in the hospital. The EP was only released in Britain in November 1971 but all of the tracks showed up a year later on the *Living In The Past* compilation LP.

In July, Jethro Tull moved to Switzerland to evade the strict UK tax laws. They were now making enough money that they felt it would be nice to keep some of it. Unfortunately, the move was difficult for the Anderson marriage, which lasted only a year. Ian and Jennie separated and were eventually divorced.

Since the music press had forced the 'concept album' label onto *Aqualung*, Ian Anderson felt that the next Tull piece should be a fully-blown, pull-out-the-stops, 'we'll show *them*' concept album. Conceived as a satirical treatise on the trials and tribulations of growing up in England, the 'piece' grew into a forty-minute opus divided into two parts (side one and side two of an LP). Progressive bands like Yes had been experimenting with longer song structures and Anderson was not about to be undone. 'Thick As A Brick' the song became *Thick As A Brick* the album!

Thick As A Brick

Released: UK: March 1972; US: May 1972

Track List: Thick As A Brick, Part One; Thick As A Brick, Part Two. (Composed by Ian Anderson.)

Note: A 25th anniversary CD reissued in 1997 was remastered and contained bonus tracks 'Thick As A Brick—Live At Madison Square Garden 1978' and 'An Interview With Ian Anderson, Martin Barre And Jeffrey Hammond.' The limited edition CD packaging replicated the original LP newspaper cover.

Cover Art: Concept by Roy Eldridge, cover material written by Ian Anderson, Jeffrey Hammond and John Evans. *Thick As A Brick* is the greatest of all Jethro Tull covers. The first edition is lavishly packaged as a bogus small-town English newspaper, complete with news articles, a crossword puzzle, television reviews and programming notes, classified ads and photographs. It even features a 'review' of the *Thick As A Brick* album! The entire thing is done in a humorous, zany style that captures the antics of *The Goon Show* or *Monty Python's Flying Circus*. In the first few pressings of the LP, the newspaper ran several pages; unfortunately, future pressings dispensed with the bulk of it. It is perhaps the most audacious, attention-getting package for a rock LP to date.

Personnel: Ian Anderson (vocals, flute, acoustic guitar, violin, saxophone, trumpet); Martin Barre (electric guitar, lute); John Evan (piano, Hammond organ, harpsichord); Jeffrey Hammond-Hammond (bass guitar, vocals); Barriemore Barlow (drums, percussion, timpani). Strings arranged and conducted by David Palmer. Produced by Ian Anderson (Executive Producer Terry Ellis).

Recording Background: Rehearsed mostly in a cold, London flat in December 1971 and then recorded in marathon sessions, the album was a taxing effort on the band. Martin Barre has said that it was a monstrous chore just trying to remember what was supposed to come next. Even though the band recorded the various movements separately, they had to be able to play the entire thing live—the upcoming concert tour was going to feature *Brick* in its entirety! To accomplish this, the band had to operate as an ensemble more than ever before. They had to be *tight*. The music was extremely complex and presented unexpected time signature changes, startling shifts in dynamics and lengthy instrumental passages. If there was any doubt that Jethro Tull didn't consist of accomplished musicians, *Thick As A Brick* laid that notion to rest!

Comments: The album is a magnificent achievement. It is full of wit and whimsy, addictive melodies, awesome instrumental breaks and is structured like a piece of classical music, divided into movements. It combines elements from rock, classical, medieval, folk, jazz and even theatrical show music. There are portions of hard rock throughout the piece but in actuality it is one of the band's lighter efforts. Thematically the lyrics tackle even more diverse subjects than on *Aqualung*, as Anderson takes stabs at England's public school system, adolescence, conformity and peer pressure. It is Ian Anderson's cynicism at its best—clever, witty and dead on. In terms of the band's evolution, it's a significant departure from previous Tull music as well as a departure from the rock music genre. *Thick As A Brick* is one of the albums that truly defines the Progressive Rock school. Following its release, other bands attempted to do epic-length pieces; some were successful but none reached the apex achieved by Jethro Tull.

Trivia: The piece is touted as being written by a twelve-year-old prodigy named Gerald Bostock. His picture adorns the cover of the album. This was all a hoax, of course, and it wasn't long before everyone knew that it was Ian Anderson who had composed it. The phrase 'thick as a brick' is a North England expression meaning someone with very little brains ("That guy is thick as a brick!"). The album was the band's first #1 hit in America and it reached #5 in the UK.

Verdict: Arguably the best Jethro Tull album ever. It is a work of unqualified genius. 5/5

The *Thick As A Brick* tour was a theatrical extravaganza rivalled only by huge supergroups such as The Who and Pink Floyd. In many ways it was like a Monty Python concert with Jethro Tull music. The band members were in and out of costumes, sight gags abounded, roadies appeared dressed in head-to-toe rabbit outfits and an on-stage telephone rang in the middle of a song, interrupting the band. Many of these gags became standard, running jokes and still pop up in Jethro Tull concerts to this day. The entire opus was performed first without a break, after which Ian Anderson drew a huge laugh when he said, "For our next number…"

The next Jethro Tull album was a 2-LP compilation but it belongs here in the discussion of new albums simply because much of it was previously unavailable on LPs and nearly all of it was unknown to American audiences.

Living In The Past

Released: UK: June 1972; US: October 1972

Track List: A Song For Jeffrey (from *This Was*); Love Story; A Christmas Song; Living In The Past; Driving Song; Bourée (from *Stand Up*); Sweet Dream; Singing All Day; Teacher (version #2); The Witch's Promise; Inside (from *Benefit*)*; Alive And Well And Living In (from *Benefit*); Just Trying To Be; By Kind Permission Of (recorded live at Carnegie Hall, 1970); Dharma For One (recorded live at Carnegie Hall, 1970); Wond'ring Again (previously unreleased); Hymn 43 (from *Aqualung*)*; Locomotive Breath (from *Aqualung*)*; Life Is A Long Song; Up The Pool; Dr Bogenbroom; From Later; Nursie. (All songs by Ian Anderson except 'Bourée' by J. S. Bach, 'By Kind Permission Of' by John Evan and 'Dharma For One' by Ian Anderson and Clive Bunker.)

* The UK and US releases had different track listings. The UK edition omitted 'Alive And Well And Living In' and 'Hymn 43.' The US edition omitted 'Inside' and 'Locomotive Breath.'

Note: Both UK and US CD releases consist of one disk, omitting 'Bourée' and 'Teacher.' A Mobile High Fidelity CD reissue in 1997 is packaged with two disks and combines both the UK and US editions so that every track from both countries is represented. Naturally, this version is the CD edition to buy!

Cover Art: Designed by CCS. *Living In The Past* has another lavishly designed LP package. Made to look like a photo album (complete with thick cardboard, embossed front and back covers and several pages in between), the product is gorgeous to look at and quite heavy. The inner pages are filled with glossy colour photographs of the band members from 1968 to 1972. The two LPs fit in sleeves that are bound in with the pages.

Personnel: All of the various line-ups of Jethro Tull since 1968 are represented. Produced by Ian Anderson and Terry Ellis.

Recording Background: With Jethro Tull's huge success worldwide, especially in America, Chrysalis decided to put together a compilation consisting of existing album tracks, previously unreleased tracks, live material and rare singles and B-sides. American audiences, for example, had not heard the *Life Is A Long Song* EP and it is included in its entirety here. 'Singing All Day' is an out-take from the 'Sweet Dream' single recording sessions. 'Wond'ring Again' is an out-take from the *Aqualung* sessions. The two long cuts from the November 1970 Carnegie Hall concert fill one complete side of an LP.

Comments: A wonderful collection and, at the time, an excellent retrospective of the band's short history and rise to stardom. Listening to 'A Song For Jeffrey,' the album's opener, one immediately realises how primitive it sounds compared to what comes later. The Carnegie Hall material is a delight and it only makes fans crave more. (In another 21 years the rest of the concert would be made available.) Ian Anderson's growth as a composer and lyricist is strikingly apparent as the album moves chronologically from the bluesy *This Was* period up to *Thick As A Brick.* Nearly all the tracks are highlights, even the obscure B-sides like the funky 'Driving Song' or the instrumental 'From Later.'

Trivia: The album hit #8 in the UK and #3 in the US. John Evans' 'By Kind Permission Of' affectionately pays homage to Beethoven's 'Piano Sonata No. 8 in C minor, Opus 13,' Claude Debussy's 'Golliwog's Cakewalk' and other classical piano pieces. The album is the first to feature the Chrysalis Records label. With the sales of this album, Ian Anderson was able to purchase a new house for his parents.

Verdict: Because much of the album is unavailable elsewhere except on rare singles, it is a must-have. 5/5

In late summer of 1972, Jethro Tull went to record a new album at the Château d'Hérouville studio in Paris, France. It was to be another concept album, this time two LPs in length. About three-quarters of it was laid down but Ian Anderson ultimately scrapped the entire thing. From then on, these 'lost' tapes became known as the 'Chateau D'Isaster Tapes,' because Anderson wasn't happy with the material. Only two tracks were salvaged, 'Only Solitaire' and 'Skating Away On The Thin

Ice Of A New Day,' both of which appeared on an album two years later. Fans eventually learned of the 'Chateau D'Isaster Tapes' and for years made bids for them to be released. Finally, in 1988, three tracks were unveiled on the *20 Years Of Jethro Tull* box set and then in 1993, many more were released on the compilation *Nightcap*.

The band returned to England, ending their one-year tax exile in Switzerland, and began working on a completely new album that borrowed some musical motifs and thematic material from the scrapped Paris album.

A Passion Play

Released: July 1973

Track List: A Passion Play, Part One; The Story Of The Hare Who Lost His Spectacles; A Passion Play, Part Two. (Composed by Ian Anderson; 'The Story Of The Hare Who Lost His Spectacles' written by Jeffrey Hammond-Hammond, John Evan and Ian Anderson.)

Note: The Mobile High Fidelity CD reissue in 1998 divides the album into the following tracks for the first time: Lifebeats; Prelude; The Silver Cord; Re-Assuring Tune; Memory Bank; Best Friends; Critique Oblique; Forest Dance #1; The Story Of The Hare Who Lost His Spectacles; Forest Dance #2; The Foot Of The Stairs; Overseer Overture; Flight From Lucifer; 10:08 From Paddington; Magus Perde; Epilogue.

Cover Art: Designed by Jennifer Ann and Geoffrey Dowlatshahi. Another satirical and extravagant LP cover for Jethro Tull, this time a mock theatre playbill with the band members featured as the play's actors. Inside jokes abound in the fake actor bios. The complete album lyrics are reprinted in a gatefold superimposed over comedy/tragedy masks. The front cover features a photograph of a ballerina lying dead on the stage; on the back cover she is alive and dancing.

Personnel: Ian Anderson (vocals, flute, acoustic guitar, soprano and sopranino saxophones); Martin Barre (electric guitar); Jeffrey Hammond-Hammond (bass guitar, vocals); John Evan (piano, Hammond organ, synthesisers, speech); Barriemore Barlow (drums, timpani, glockenspiel, marimba). Orchestra arranged and conducted by David Palmer. Produced by Ian Anderson.

Recording Background: After the so-called 'Chateau D'Isaster Tapes' were abandoned, Jethro Tull quickly assembled another concept album. Since *Thick As A Brick* had been such a success, why not do another one? This time, however, Ian Anderson wrote a very serious piece about life and death. Culling thematic elements from Dante and medieval passion plays, the opus became something of a Jethro Tull's Inferno. To bring a little levity to the proceedings, a piece entitled 'The Story Of The Hare Who Lost His Spectacles' was inserted in the middle. This was a mock children's story that is told by Jeffrey Hammond in a silly Monty Python-style voice (in concert, it was accompanied by a film starring the band and other actors dressed in animal costumes).

Comments: A Passion Play is a major turning point for Jethro Tull. On the positive side, it's the most ambitious, complex and groundbreaking album they ever recorded. Musically and lyrically it goes way beyond most preconceived ideas of what a rock album is supposed to be and that may be why the press savaged it. *A Passion Play* is in actuality a piece of modern classical music. It just happens to contain passages of rock and jazz. It is an album that requires repeated listenings to fully appreciate. It is a difficult, challenging piece of art that exhibits massive doses of intelligence and creativity but the problem is that it is perhaps too serious and highbrow for the mass population of folks that normally purchase albums by rock bands. The melodies are unusual and the instrumental passages are eccentric. If it were really a stage play, one wouldn't leave the theatre humming the tunes. That said, the album's strengths must be pointed out. Ian Anderson's voice is the best it's ever been or ever will be. The vocals on *A Passion Play* are spellbinding; it was as if Homer had risen from the grave and was relating a magical tale in a cryptic, mysterious narrative. The overall sound of the band is different as well. There are more instruments present, specifically synthesisers and saxophones. The synthesisers add a level to the music that almost makes you think you're listening to a completely new band. It's only when Anderson sings and plays the flute that we know it's Jethro Tull. 'The Story of the Hare Who Lost His Spectacles' is totally weird and amusing in a way, but it may have been too British to be fully appreciated by American audiences. It comes off as simply strange. Production values are top notch.

Trivia: The album gave the band its second #1 album in the US. It reached #13 in the UK.

Verdict: I feel that *A Passion Play* is definitely one of Jethro Tull's absolute best albums. However, I do find myself wavering on where it stands in the upper echelon of their works. For years I felt that it was second only to *Thick As A Brick*, but this opinion has changed. Hence, I give it… 4/5

The tour that accompanied *A Passion Play* was another no-holds-barred theatrical production that ran nearly three hours in length. A full multimedia event, the show featured several costume changes and special effects. It didn't go well. One of the problems was that the tour began before the album had actually been released, so the audiences had no idea what they were about to see and hear. Since the material was difficult and uncompromising, the response was not great. Of course, there were some that loved every minute but unfortunately *A Passion Play* became the pivotal work that alienated the rock music press and divided Tull's fans.

WarChild

Released: October 1974

Track List: WarChild; Queen And Country; Ladies; Back-Door Angels; Sea Lion; Skating Away On The Thin Ice Of A New Day; Bungle In The Jungle; Only Solitaire; The Third Hoorah; Two Fingers. (All songs by Ian Anderson.)

Cover Art: Designed by Shirtsleeves Studio. A simpler album cover than usual with a photographic negative of Ian Anderson holding a 'WarChild' sceptre/banner and assuming an aggressive pose. A city skyscape is in the background. Printed as a single sleeve, the back cover features a collage of the band members and others in costumes, illustrating the various songs on the album. For example, a Renaissance-costumed Jeffrey Hammond is seen bowing to Queen Elizabeth ('Queen and Country').

Personnel: Ian Anderson (vocals, flute, acoustic guitar, alto, soprano and sopranino saxophones); Martin Barre (electric and Spanish guitars); Jeffrey Hammond-Hammond (bass guitar, string bass); John Evan (piano, Hammond organ, synthesisers, piano accordion); Barriemore Barlow (drums, glockenspiel, marimba, percussion.) Strings arranged and conducted by David Palmer. Philamusica of London led by Patrick Halling. Produced by Ian Anderson (Executive Producer Terry Ellis). Recording Engineer: Robin Black.

Recording Background: The critical response to *A Passion Play* led to a mysterious (and untrue) press release by Chrysalis Records stating that Jethro Tull was retiring from touring! The band was incensed because they had no intention of retiring. Ian Anderson had turned his attention to the possibility of creating a Jethro Tull motion picture entitled *WarChild*. It was to have an orchestral soundtrack, with Anderson composing it in close collaboration with David Palmer. Numerous delays and financial difficulties in getting the project off the ground forced Anderson to abandon the idea and simply make a new Jethro Tull album incorporating the ideas that were to be in the film. Two of the songs on the album ('Skating Away' and 'Only Solitaire') had been recorded in 1972 as part of the 'Chateau D'Isaster' Tapes, but the rest were recorded in 1974. Several other songs from the sessions didn't surface until years later.

Comments: Reverting to a song-based structure, *WarChild* eschews the epic-length pieces of the last two studio albums. The overall sound of the album is similar to *A Passion Play* with the prominence of John Evans' synthesisers. As for the songs, they are a very good bunch with clever and witty lyrics. The familiar Anderson cynicism is back, this time with a vengeance (for example, 'Only Solitaire' is a direct slam at rock critics and 'Queen And Country' criticises British imperialism). 'Bungle In The Jungle' became a US top-forty hit single and is a pleasant and silly song—almost a novelty record—but it has no business being grouped in the same category of Tull classic singles such as 'Living In The Past' or 'The Witch's Promise.' 'Skating Away On The Thin Ice Of A New Day' is a highlight with the band playing an assortment of unusual instruments (glockenspiel, accordion, etc.) in a cornucopia of English, Russian and Indian influences. *WarChild* is a return to form, more or less, redeeming the band in the eyes of those that didn't care for *A Passion Play*.

Trivia: The song 'Two Fingers' is a reworking of 'Lick Your Fingers Clean,' the out-take that was rejected from *Aqualung*. The album was a big hit in the US, reaching #2; it got to #14 in the UK.

Verdict: A very good, enjoyable Tull album with all the right elements in all the right places. Personally, I don't feel that they needed to 'redeem' themselves for *A Passion Play*, which is a far more challenging album. *WarChild*, though, is one of the best of the middle-tier albums. 3/5

Like the album, the WarChild tour was very successful. A string quartet was hired to accompany the band and they were dressed in platinum wigs and Beethoven-esque clothing. Ian Anderson sported a minstrel costume, complete with codpiece. The Monty Python-style gags continued to infiltrate the proceedings, the music was tight, the band was colourful and thus the overall vibe was festive and exhilarating. During the performance of 'Sea Lion,' a large balloon was brought on stage and bounced into the audience. This device grew thematically and eventually it became a tradition for two large balloons to be used at every Jethro Tull show's finale. During the final song, roadies hand off a massive balloon to Anderson, who balances it on his head for a few minutes, then knocks it over the audience. A second balloon follows. The balloons are bounced around the venue until they invariably burst.

Minstrel In The Gallery

Released: September 1975

Track List: Minstrel In The Gallery; Cold Wind To Valhalla; Black Satin Dancer; Requiem; One White Duck/0^{10} = Nothing At All; Baker St. Muse: a. Pig Me And The Whore; b. Nice Little Tune; c. Crash Barrier Waltzer; d. Mother England Reverie; Grace. (All songs by Ian Anderson.)

Cover Art: Artwork by R. Kriss and J. Garnett, based on a print by Joseph Nash. A simple and tasteful single sleeve cover, showing a medieval portrait of a troupe of minstrels performing for royalty. The back cover is a Brian Ward colour photo of the band looking down from a 'gallery' above a stage.

Personnel: Ian Anderson (vocals, flute, acoustic guitar); Martin Barre (electric guitar); Jeffrey Hammond-Hammond (bass guitar, string bass); John Evan (piano, Hammond organ); Barriemore Barlow (drums, percussion). With guests Patrick Halling (violin leader); Elizabeth Edwards, Rita Eddows, Bridget Procter (violins); Katherine Thulborn (cello). Strings arranged and conducted by David Palmer. Produced by Ian Anderson. Recording Engineer: Robin Black.

Recording Background: Recorded in Monte Carlo with the band's new mobile studio, the songs on the album reflected Ian Anderson's restlessness, anger and unhappiness with his personal life at the time, the press, the constant touring and responsibilities of being the band's leader and, it must be said, the band itself. Anderson went on the record saying that the group members were unhappy and weren't functioning well as a unit. As for himself, Anderson was tired of being single and living alone. The photographs of Anderson and the band on the LP's inner sleeve indeed show a bunch of guys who *look* tired—there are bags under their eyes, they are rather haggard and appear as if they've been up for days.

Comments: Despite the malaise that accompanied the recording of the album, *Minstrel In The Gallery* is a fabulous LP. It's true that the songs are more introspective, darker and extremely personal and this is precisely why they're good. It's a very *moving* album. Musically, it alternates between hard, clashing rock and acoustic, quiet numbers. The title song is an excellent rocker and was released as a single. 'Cold Wind To Valhalla' is a vigorous and delightful tune with the usual eclectic mix of instrumentation. 'Black Satin Dancer' tends to drag a bit and brings down the LP's first side. The highlight and centrepiece of the album is the epic 'Baker St. Muse,' which takes up nearly all of the second side of the original LP. Once again working within the framework of a suite with separate movements, Anderson presents a complex and multi-layered piece that stands as one of the best things he has ever done.

Trivia: The album reached #7 in the US and #20 in the UK.

Verdict: On the strength of 'Baker St. Muse' alone, the album belongs in the top ten. But because of some weaker parts in the first half, I give it… 4/5

After nearly five years of playing bass for Jethro Tull, Jeffrey Hammond decided to go back to his initial interest of painting. He also wanted to get married and settle down, much like Clive Bunker did before him. His replacement was a seasoned musician named John Glascock (born 2 May 1951). Glascock had been a band member of The Juniors, The Gods, Head Machine, Chicken Shack, The Bee Gees, Carmen and others.

Too Old To Rock 'N' Roll—Too Young To Die!

Released: UK: April 1976; US: May 1976

Track List: Quizz Kid; Crazed Institution; Salamander; Taxi Grab; From A Dead Beat To An Old Greazer; Bad-Eyed And Loveless; Big Dipper; Too Old To Rock 'N' Roll—Too Young To Die; Pied Piper; The Chequered Flag (Dead Or Alive). (All songs by Ian Anderson.)

Cover Art: Designed and illustrated by Michael Farrell and David Gibbons. A gatefold cover, the album features comic strip artwork that illustrates the story behind the album. The cover features Ian Anderson as 'Ray Lomas,' the protagonist, shaking his fist at us (actually he's saying, "F**k you!").

Personnel: Ian Anderson (vocals, flute, acoustic and electric guitars, harmonica, percussion); Martin Barre (electric and acoustic guitars); John Evan (piano); John Glascock (bass guitar, vocals); Barriemore Barlow (drums, percussion). With guests: David Palmer (saxophone, Vako Orchestron, string arrangements), Maddy Prior and Angela Allen (backing vocals). Produced by Ian Anderson.

Recording Background: The album came about after plans to create a stage musical fell apart. Anderson and David Palmer had written a story about an ageing rocker who has gone out of favour, has a motorcycle accident and suddenly regains popularity. It was being written for 60s pop star Adam Faith but like so many endeavours in show business the project never got off the ground. Like the *WarChild* film, the stage musical was channelled into a new Jethro Tull album. John Glascock made his debut with Tull on this LP.

Comments: Too Old To Rock 'N' Roll is an underrated album. Generally speaking, it's an upbeat record, certainly more optimistic than *Minstrel In The Gallery* and the songs have a more commercial feel than much of what Tull has produced before. There are several very good songs with strong melodies and hooks, such as 'Quizz Kid,' 'Crazed Institution,' 'Taxi Grab' and the title song. A major highlight is the slow tempo ballad, 'From A Dead Beat To An Old Greazer,' one of Anderson's most haunting songs. 'Salamander' is an excellent acoustic guitar number typical of Tull's quieter moments. The rest of the album, however, is middle-of-the road but certainly not terrible. The real problem is the mix. The sound is muddy and dampened; one has to crank up the volume to really hear the nuances. If there were ever a Tull album that needs remastering, this is it.

Trivia: The album reached #23 in the UK and #14 in the US.

Verdict: The songs are melodic, catchy and fun. Not a masterpiece by any means but a good middle-tier album. 3/5

At the end of 1976, Jethro Tull released a UK-only EP of four original Christmas songs: 'Ring Out, Solstice Bells,' which was new and would also feature on the next LP release; 'March, the Mad Scientist,' recorded in 1974; 'A Christmas Song,' the original 1968 version; and 'Pan Dance,' an instrumental also from 1974. Ian Anderson has said that Christmas was a special time of the year for him and several songs from the Tull catalogue would continue to reflect this sentiment.

4: Salmon Farmer
And Rock Star (1977 – 1979)

Ian Anderson married Shona Learoyd in late 1976 and they moved into a 630-acre farmhouse estate in Buckinghamshire. By now, all of the band members had moved out of the city and were indulging in the rustic pleasures of country life. This attitude was explored in the band's next album.

Songs From The Wood

Released: February 1977

Track List: Songs From The Wood; Jack In The Green; Cup Of Wonder; Hunting Girl; Ring Out, Solstice Bells; Velvet Green; The Whistler; Pibroch (Cap In Hand); Fire At Midnight. (All songs by Ian Anderson; additional material by David Palmer and Martin Barre; arrangements by Jethro Tull.)

Cover Art: The front cover of the single-sleeve LP features a painting by Jay L. Lee of Ian Anderson by a campfire in the woods. The back cover painting by Shirtsleeve Studio is a tree trunk with grooves drawn on the flattened top and a phonograph arm/needle attached to it.

Personnel: Ian Anderson (vocals, flute, acoustic and electric guitars, mandolin, tin whistles, percussion); Martin Barre (electric guitar, lute); John Evan (piano, Hammond organ, synthesisers); John Glascock (bass guitar); David Palmer (piano, synthesisers, portative organ); Barriemore Barlow (drums, glockenspiel, bells, nakers, tabor). Produced by Ian Anderson. Recording engineers: Robin Black, Thing Moss and Trevor White.

Recording Background: The move out of the city and into the country apparently rubbed off on Ian Anderson and company in a positive way. The album reflected his new outlook and featured songs that are optimistic, full of life and simply uplifting. Recorded in late 1976, Anderson allowed the band to come up with many of the arrangements and the addition of David Palmer into the mix raised the bar considerably. Though he has denied that it was intentional, Anderson managed to come up with a wholly-British LP that drew on a wide spectrum of British cultural history and musical roots—Renaissance, Scottish folk, English folk, rock and classical music.

Comments: Easily one of the five best Jethro Tull albums, *Songs From The Wood* is a masterpiece of British Progressive Rock that actually belies that label. So many diverse styles and elements come together in the work that it is impossible to accurately categorise. Arguably, the title track could stand as Jethro Tull's greatest single song. The vocal harmonies, quirky time signatures and amazing lead guitar/flute/keyboards interchange in the middle combine to create an awesome opening to the LP. Each successive song continues the high level of quality until, at the end, one is left panting with elation. 'Jack In The Green' is a sprightly song about little green fairies that live in the forest. 'Hunting Girl' gallops along with an infectious rhythm and tight harmonies. 'Velvet Green' is another song with numerous time signature changes and a Gothic atmosphere. 'The Whistler' (also released as a single in the UK) is a magnificent piece showcasing Anderson's flute and also his expertise on the tin whistle. 'Pibroch' is another Jethro Tull mini-epic full of medieval motifs and impressive Martin Barre guitar work. In short, every song is a gem. Released at a time when punk rock and new wave was taking over the commercial music scene, *Songs From The Wood* managed to be a big hit and deservedly so.

Trivia: The word 'Pibroch' is Anglicised Gaelic meaning a tune played on bagpipes. The album reached #13 in the UK and #8 in the US.

Verdict: Brilliant. It sounds just as fresh today as it did in 1977. 5/5

After a successful tour around the world throughout most of the year, Anderson bought a second country home, this time the 15,300-acre Strathaird Estate on the Isle of Skye in northern Scotland. This act led Anderson to become interested in the possibility of operating a salmon farm on the property. Practically teaching himself how to do it from books, Anderson produced the salmon at Strathaird and developed smoking and processing plants in Inverness. The enterprise grew from a small four-man business to a corporation employing over four hundred people. Strathaird Salmon Ltd. became such a success that the local residents nicknamed Anderson 'The Laird of Strathaird' since he had created so many jobs in the area. By the mid-80s, the company would be one of the most successful, if not *the* most successful, salmon farming operation in Britain. The notion that the words 'rock star' and 'salmon farmer' could describe the same person merely added a new level to Ian Anderson's mystique.

Heavy Horses

Released: April 1978

Track List: ...And The Mouse Police Never Sleeps; Acres Wild; No Lullaby; Moths; Journeyman; Rover; One Brown Mouse; Heavy Horses; Weathercock. (All songs by Ian Anderson.)

Cover Art: James Cotier's colour photograph adorns the front of this LP, featuring Ian Anderson in a country squire's outfit, leading two horses by the reins. Shona Anderson's picturesque back cover photograph shows the band lounging in what appears to be a country manor.

Personnel: Ian Anderson (vocals, flute, acoustic and electric guitars, mandolin); Martin Barre (electric and acoustic guitars); John Glascock (bass guitar); John Evan (piano, Hammond organ); David Palmer (portative organ, keyboards, string arrangements); Barriemore Barlow (drums, percussion). With guest: Darryl Way (violin). Produced by Ian Anderson. Recording engineer: Robin Black.

Recording Background: Jethro Tull continued its excursion into the rustic themes explored in the previous album. Much of *Heavy Horses* was recorded in Anderson's own recording studio, Maison Rouge, in South London. The band laid down enough songs for two records, but half of them were scrapped because they were considered inferior. The ones that remained for the album are very good, creating an LP nearly as compelling as *Songs From The Wood.* Anderson described the album as *Songs From The Wood, Part II,* 'with a little more Jethro Tull.'

Comments: The album is less optimistic, darker and more menacing than its predecessor but that's not necessarily a bad thing. One song is too long and tends to drag down the first half of the album ('No Lullaby') and a couple of tunes simply aren't very strong ('Journeyman,' 'Weathercock'). Otherwise, *Heavy Horses* is a worthy successor to the previous hit LP and it is a firm favourite with fans. Many of the songs deal with animals—mice, cats, horses, roosters, moths—with one song inspired by Scot poet Robert Burns ('One Brown Mouse'). Major highlights include 'Acres Wild,' with guest Darryl Way's violin jigging along nicely; the melodious 'Moths' (released as a single in the UK); 'Rover,' a semi-ballad with an Old English feel that is my personal favourite on the LP; the playful 'One Brown Mouse'; and the title track, which became a concert standard and is still played today.

Trivia: The album reached #20 in the UK and #19 in the US.

Verdict: A solid entry in the Tull catalogue. 4/5

Shortly after the European leg of the *Heavy Horses* tour, John Glascock became seriously ill from complications arising from a tooth infection. The infection spread to his heart, which already had a weak valve—something he apparently inherited from his father. To save his life, he had to undergo heart surgery in the fall of 1978. Tull was scheduled to go on tour in America at that time, so the band had to find a temporary replacement on bass. The job went to Tony Williams, a Blackpool resident and friend of the old John Evan Band members. A highlight of the tour included a performance at Madison Square Garden in New York that became the first live worldwide satellite broadcast of a rock concert on television and radio.

Bursting Out—Jethro Tull Live

Released: September 1978

Track List: No Lullaby; Sweet Dream; Skating Away On The Thin Ice Of A New Day; Jack In The Green; One Brown Mouse; A New Day Yesterday; Flute Solo Improvisation/God Rest Ye Merry Gentlemen/Bourée; Songs From the Wood; Thick As A Brick; Hunting Girl; Too Old To Rock 'N' Roll—Too Young To Die; Conundrum; Minstrel In The Gallery; Cross-Eyed Mary; Quatrain; Aqualung; Locomotive Breath; The Dambuster's March. All songs by Ian Anderson except 'God Rest Ye Merry Gentlemen' (traditional), 'Bourée' (J. S. Bach), 'Conundrum' (Barre), 'Quatrain' (Barre), 'Aqualung' (I. Anderson/J. Anderson) and 'The Dambuster's March' (Eric Coates).

Note: The US CD version of the album is heavily edited to fit on one disk. The UK version is a 2-CD set and contains the complete album.

Cover Art: Design by Ramey Communications. Colour photographs of the band by Brian Cooke and Ruan O'Lochlainn adorn the gatefold double LP. The front cover features Ian Anderson beneath one of the giant balloons that are traditionally bounced into the audience at a show's finale.

Personnel: Ian Anderson (vocals, flute, acoustic guitar); Martin Barre (electric guitar, mandolin, marimba); John Glascock (bass guitar, electric guitar, vocals); John Evan (piano, Hammond organ, accordion, synthesisers); David Palmer (portative organ, synthesisers); Barriemore Barlow (drums, glockenspiel). Produced by Ian Anderson. Recorded 'somewhere in Europe' with the Maison Rouge Mobile Studio, engineers Robin Black, Christopher Amson and Pavel Kubes.

Recording Background: To celebrate Jethro Tull's 10th anniversary it was decided to record and release the band's first official live album. Recorded during the *Heavy Horses* European tour in the summer of 1978, the double LP set is culled from several concerts and features a potpourri of tunes representing the band's history (although nothing from *This Was* is included). Two original instrumental numbers by Martin Barre are incorporated. The version of 'Thick As A Brick' is an abridged medley that uses roughly 2/3 of Part One from the original album. (Through the years, the band's live rendition of 'Thick As A Brick' would become shorter and shorter until it reached a mere six or seven minutes.) A studio-recorded single, 'A Stitch In Time,' was released in conjunction with the album, backed by the live version of 'Sweet Dream.'

Comments: As far as live albums go, this one is very good. The sound quality is excellent and the crowd noise is filtered down to a minimum. There is a school of thought that studio albums are always better than live albums and I'm afraid I'm one of those sticklers. I would much rather listen to the originals unless I'm at the concert in person! That said, *Bursting Out* is an excellent representation of what Jethro Tull sounded like in 1978. Ian Anderson's banter between songs is always amusing and entertaining. Martin Barre shines throughout the proceedings, especially on his two solo tracks. Highlights include: 'Skating Away,' 'A New Day Yesterday,' 'Thick as a Brick,' 'Hunting Girl,' 'Conundrum,' 'Minstrel In The Gallery' and what is perhaps the best live version of 'Aqualung' available.

Trivia: The album reached #17 in the UK, the first time a Tull album beat the chart position in America (#21) since *Aqualung*!

Verdict: An excellent live album but I'm partial to studio recordings. 3/5

Robin Anderson, Ian's brother and general administrator for The Scottish Ballet, had the idea of opening the new Glasgow theatre with an original work by contemporary composers. Conceived as a three-part ballet, the first two acts were to be written by rock stars and the third act would utilise the music of Duke Ellington. Jon Anderson (no relation), the lead singer of Yes, was responsible for the first act. Ian Anderson, working with David Palmer and Martin Barre, wrote the second act, which came to be called *The Water's Edge*. Due to a number of misfortunes, mostly a lack of adequate rehearsal time, the ballet was a failure. Anderson put the ordeal behind him and Jethro Tull went on a short American tour in the spring of 1979. John Glascock was back in the band, but he hadn't fully recovered from his heart surgery. He began to experience circulation problems and by the time the group returned to England to record the next LP, Glascock could barely play his instrument.

Stormwatch

Released: September 1979

Track List: North Sea Oil; Orion; Home; Dark Ages; Warm Sporran; Something's On The Move; Old Ghosts; Dun Ringill; Flying Dutchman; Elegy. (All songs by Ian Anderson, except 'Elegy' by David Palmer; arrangements by Jethro Tull.)

Cover Art: Conceived by Ian Anderson, art direction by Peter Wagg, cover painting by David Jackson. A close-up, scary-looking Ian Anderson peers out from behind binoculars on the cover of the album. He's apparently in a cold climate, dressed in a parka and gloves. Lightning is reflected in the binocular lenses. A polar bear looms over a nuclear power plant on the back cover.

Personnel: Ian Anderson (vocals, flute, acoustic guitar, bass guitar); Martin Barre (electric and classical guitars, mandolin); John Evan (piano, Hammond organ, synthesisers); David Palmer (synthesisers, portative organ, string arrangements); Barriemore Barlow (drums, percussion). With John Glascock (bass guitar on 'Orion,' 'Flying Dutchman' and 'Elegy') and Francis Wilson (narration on 'Dun Ringill'). Produced by Ian Anderson. Recording engineers: Robin Black and Leigh Mantle.

Recording History: John Glascock was not doing well. He was able to play on a few songs, three of which were ultimately included on the album. Ian Anderson had to take up the bass and play the parts intended for Glascock. *Stormwatch* made up the third part of the informal 'rustic' trilogy that began with *Songs From The Wood*. Just as *Heavy Horses* had been darker and not as optimistic, *Stormwatch* went even further—the album was seeped with Ian Anderson cynicism. This time his pessimism was directed toward man's treatment of the environment. As Anderson was now a salmon farmer, his interest in ecological matters blossomed in the new song set. There were also a couple of songs dealing with maritime themes, prompting the use of ship riggings as set decoration on the subsequent tour. The doom and gloom atmosphere of the album was also present in the studio. The current band line-up was unhappy again. Barrie Barlow was reportedly at odds with Anderson, Glascock was missed and John Evan was drinking heavily and suffering from depression. All of this would come to a head during the upcoming tour.

Comments: A lot of fans have a fondness for this album but I don't. The cynical issues and dark qualities of the music create a cold and austere mood that is simply not conducive to the Jethro Tull we know and love. Some songs are too long and are frankly boring ('Dark Ages,' 'Flying Dutchman') and a couple are uninspired ('Orion,' 'Old Ghosts'). On the plus side, David Palmer's 'Elegy' is a lovely instrumental piece originally used in *The Water's Edge* ballet; 'North Sea Oil' is a punchy tune that was released as a single; 'Warm Sporran' has a nice groove; and 'Dun Ringill' could possibly be the most hypnotic song in the Tull catalogue. In fact, 'Dun Ringill' is the best thing on the record. The song concerns a secret hilltop haven on Anderson's Scottish estate where he often goes to brood and reflect as the weather rages around him.

Trivia: The album reached #27 in the UK and #22 in the US.

Verdict: The album has its moments but mostly it seems uninspired. 1/5

It was apparent that John Glascock was too ill to continue playing with Jethro Tull. The *Stormwatch* tour was imminent, so another personnel change had to be made. The new bassist was Dave Pegg (born 2 November 1947), a seasoned musician who had spent most of his career with the folk-oriented band Fairport Convention. His first task with Tull was to record a piece entitled 'King Henry's Madrigal,' which was used as a theme for a BBC arts program called *Mainstream*. The song was released on a rare EP in the UK that included two songs from *Stormwatch* and a reprise of 'Ring Out, Solstice Bells.' Pegg then set off with the band for the fall 1979 tour.

Morale on the tour was at an all-time low. Once again, the band simply didn't gel. Audience attendance was also noticeably reduced, which didn't help matters. There was a feeling in the group that Jethro Tull's time was up. New Wave and other styles of music were at the forefront and it appeared that no one but the die-hard fans cared.

News of John Glascock's death compounded the situation. The musician died on 17 November 1979 after his body had rejected his new heart valve. The band members were devastated but gallantly carried on with the final shows before returning home. Once back in England, it was clear that the current Tull line-up was splintering. Barrie Barlow indicated that he would be leaving the band to form his own group. John Evan had a drinking problem. David Palmer was looking into other musical endeavours.

The close of the decade also brought an end to an era in the Jethro Tull history book.

5: New Decade, New Directions (1980 – 1990)

It was time for a change. With unrest brewing within the band, Ian Anderson decided that perhaps it was a good moment to make that solo album that fans, as well as Chrysalis Records, had been clamouring for. Intent on working with a new set of musicians, Anderson put Jethro Tull on temporary hiatus and enlisted the services of Eddie Jobson (born 28 April 1955), former keyboard player and violinist with Curved Air, Roxy Music, Frank Zappa and the band U.K. U.k. had supported Tull during the Heavy Horses tour and Anderson was impressed with Jobson's talent. For a drummer, Jobson's pal Mark Craney (born 15 August 1952) was enlisted. Dave Pegg was kept on as bass player and it wasn't until the last minute that Martin Barre was asked to complete the line-up on electric guitar. After the album was recorded, Barrie Barlow, John Evans and David Palmer were dismissed from Jethro Tull. The three musicians were surprised, to say the least and Barlow and Evans, especially, took it hard. Apparently it was decided by both Anderson and Chrysalis that the new album would be credited not to Ian Anderson as a solo effort, but as Jethro Tull's new LP.

"A"

Released: UK: August 1980; US: September 1980

Track List: Crossfire; Fylingdale Flyer; Working John, Working Joe; Black Sunday; Protect And Survive; Batteries Not Included; Uniform; 4 W.D. (Low Ratio); The Pine Marten's Jig; And Further On. (All songs by Ian Anderson; additional material by Eddie Jobson.)

Cover Art: Conceived by Ian Anderson, art direction by Peter Wagg, photography by John Shaw. This unorthodox single sleeve cover has a science fiction theme with the band members dressed in white flight suits, looking out the window of a control room. They are gawking at a bright red, flying "A" in the sky. On the back cover, the band members stand on the tarmac of what appears to be an airfield, looking up in the sky with expressions of awe on their faces à la *Close Encounters Of The Third Kind*. Weird.

Personnel: Ian Anderson (vocals, flute, acoustic guitar, mandolin); Martin Barre (electric guitar); Dave Pegg (bass guitar); Eddie Jobson (keyboards, electric violin); Mark Craney (drums, percussion). Produced by Ian Anderson. Recording engineers: Robin Black, Leigh Mantle.

Recording Background: It was an uneasy time for Jethro Tull. With the dismantling of the previous line-up, no one knew for certain what the future of the group might be. After assembling the new band and recording the new material in the summer of 1980, the result was not what one might expect from an Ian Anderson solo album. Thus, Anderson threw caution to the wind and credited the album to 'Jethro Tull' and a new chapter in the band's history was begun. While the songs are credited to Anderson, new keyboard player and violinist Eddie Jobson contributed much to the instrumentation and arrangements.

Comments: This is a Tull album like no other. The most striking aspect is the overall sound—the music is very *electronic*, futuristic and, frankly, antiseptic. Jobson's synthesisers dominate the album and if it weren't for Anderson's distinctive voice and flute, you'd never know it was Jethro Tull. The songs, which deal thematically with the dangers of progress and threats to public safety, are a mixed bag, ranging from mediocre ('Crossfire,' 'Batteries Not Included,' 'Uniform') to interesting ('Fylingdale Flyer,' '4 W.D.') to excellent ('Black Sunday'). On the positive side, one must give Anderson credit for attempting to take the band in a completely new direction. At times the album is surprising, fresh and unique but mostly one comes away from it wondering what happened to Jethro Tull.

Trivia: The title *"A"* is not supposed to mean 'anarchy' as was originally thought. Since the project had begun as an Ian Anderson solo project, the tapes had been marked 'A.' For some reason or another, this label stuck. Once again, the album did better in the UK, charting at #25, whereas in America it reached #30.

Verdict: Simply because *"A"* is a more interesting listening experience than *Stormwatch*, I give it... 2/5

The subsequent tour was a very high-tech affair incorporating new state-of-the-art equipment and instruments. The band wore the peculiar white flight suits on stage, thus presenting a very different, 'modern' Jethro Tull, something that fans weren't accustomed to. A performance at the Hammersmith Odeon in London was filmed for posterity and much of the concert, along with some archival and studio footage, was released on the video *Slipstream* in 1982.

Sales for the new album and attendance at the concerts were down. Anderson yet again dismissed the current line-up in early 1981 and Jethro Tull withdrew from the public eye for over a year. During that time period, Anderson wrote dozens of new songs and Martin Barre pursued a hobby as a marathon runner. When Anderson was ready to start recording again, he recalled Barre, Pegg and a new drummer, Gerry Conway (born 11 September 1947), who was an acquaintance of Pegg's. The foursome recorded at least nine songs with Anderson dubbing keyboards before a new musician was hired. Peter-John Vettese (born 15 August 1956) answered an ad and auditioned. His knowledge of the new technology was a plus, so he was in the band.

The Broadsword And The Beast

Released: April 1982

Track List: Beastie; Clasp; Fallen On Hard Times; Flying Colours; Slow Marching Band; Broadsword; Pussy Willow; Watching Me, Watching You; Seal Driver; Cheerio. (All songs by Ian Anderson; additional material by Peter-John Vettese.)

Cover Art: The single sleeve LP was illustrated by Ian McCaig with calligraphy by Jim Gibson. It's a beautiful painting of Ian Anderson in a fantasy setting, wearing a cloak, sprouting wings and holding a huge broadsword. The ocean rages behind him. It's one of the more successful covers since *A Passion Play*.

Personnel: Ian Anderson (vocals, flute, acoustic guitar); Martin Barre (electric and acoustic guitars); Dave Pegg (bass guitar, mandolin, vocals); Peter-John Vettese (piano, synthesisers, vocals); Gerry Conway (drums, percussion). Produced by Paul Samwell-Smith; Recording engineers: Robin Black, Leigh Mantle.

Recording Background: After the songs had been recorded, Ian Anderson decided to bring in a fresh set of ears to produce the next Tull album. An American producer was brought in but dismissed after two weeks of work, after which Paul Samwell-Smith was hired. Samwell-Smith had played bass with the Yardbirds and had produced several of Cat Stevens' recordings, among others. The idea would be that Tull would use an outside producer on a one-shot basis to see how it went. Peter-John Vettese contributed a great deal of musical ideas and arrangements, hence his 'additional material' credit. By the spring of 1982, the band had enough songs in the can to fill two and a half LPs.

Only ten were selected to be on the new album; the others were held back and slowly released over the years as B-sides and as rare tracks on anniversary collections.

Comments: The Broadsword And The Beast is a terrific album and certainly a leap forward from the last two studio albums. The sound is more traditional Tull, even with Vettese's electronic keyboards filling out the proceedings. The overall feel is much warmer than what had occurred on the previous two LPs and nearly every song is a winner. The 'Beastie' half of the album deals with disappointment, fear and mistrust of various subjects—love, politics and monetary welfare. It's the stronger portion of the LP, with such standout tracks as the medieval 'Clasp,' the dynamic 'Flying Colours' and the grand 'Slow Marching Band,' which never fails to send chills up my spine. The 'Broadsword' half captures the fantasy elements depicted in the cover art and also deals with romance and the sea. The highlights in this portion are 'Pussy Willow,' with its memorable chorus hook, and the inventive 'Watching Me, Watching You.'

Trivia: The album reached #19 in the US but only #27 in the UK.

Verdict: One of the better ones. 4/5

The following tour was more light-hearted than the previous two. Supporting a more successful album helped and Jethro Tull appeared to be back in form. Unfortunately after the first leg, Gerry Conway became unavailable. Ex-10cc drummer Paul Burgess filled in on a temporary basis.

Once the tour was completed, Anderson spent time developing the salmon farming business and finally working on his first solo album. Recording with only one other musician, Peter-John Vettese, *Walk Into Light* was released in November 1983 (see Chapter 7). It was not what was expected, for it was very keyboard-oriented, utilising a great deal of high-tech synthesisers and drum machines. This concept was carried into the recording of the next Jethro Tull studio album.

Under Wraps

Released: UK: September 1984; US: October 1984

Track List: Lap Of Luxury; Under Wraps #1; European Legacy; Later, That Same Evening (Anderson/Vettese); Saboteur (Anderson/Vettese); Radio Free Moscow (Anderson/Vettese); Astronomy (Anderson/Vettese) [CD and cassette only]; Tundra (Anderson/Vettese) [CD and cassette only]; Nobody's Car (Anderson/Barre/Vettese); Heat (Anderson/Vettese); Under Wraps #2; Paparazzi (Anderson/Barre/Vettese); Apogee (Anderson/Vettese); Automotive Engineering (Anderson/Vettese) [CD and cassette only]; General Crossing (Anderson/Vettese) [CD and cassette only]. (All songs by Ian Anderson except where indicated.)

Cover Art: Conceived by Ian Anderson, designed by John Pasche, photographed by Trevor Key. The single sleeve LP features a clever photo of a (presumably) nude woman lounging underneath a sheet.

Personnel: Ian Anderson (vocals, flute, acoustic guitar, drum programming); Martin Barre (electric and acoustic guitars); Dave Pegg (bass guitar, mandolin, vocals); Peter-John Vettese (piano, synthesisers, vocals). Produced by Ian Anderson. Recording engineers: Ian Anderson, Martin Barre, Dave Pegg, Peter-John Vettese.

Recording Background: Fully immersed in the new technology of the day, Ian Anderson decided to continue the experimentation he had done on his solo album by creating a Jethro Tull album with no drummer. Instead, he used a drum machine that he programmed himself. This, combined with Vettese's electronics, produced yet another Tull album that sounds like no other. But unlike *"A"*, which sounded alien, futuristic and antiseptic, the atmosphere of *Under Wraps* is more of a techno-rock album with the voice and flute of Ian Anderson. One critic described it as 'Ultravox meets Jethro Tull.' Fans either loved it or hated it. The songs mostly deal with the universe of spies, espionage and working undercover. The original LP contained eleven tracks, while the CD and cassette added four more songs.

Comments: The sound of the album is unique and certainly different and therein lies its strength. The arrangements and musicality are top notch, Anderson's vocals are superb and Vettese's work shines. The drawback is that only about half the songs are truly memorable. The highlights include: the rocker 'Lap Of Luxury' (released as a single); the imaginatively-arranged 'Under Wraps #1'; the tricky 'European Legacy'; the ballad-like 'Later, That Same Evening'; the snappy 'Saboteur'; 'Radio Free Moscow' with its intricate vocals; another rocker 'Nobody's Car'; and the wonderful, acoustic 'Under Wraps #2,' which stands out because it lacks the techno qualities of the rest of the LP. It is the same song (lyrics and melody) as 'Under Wraps #1,' except that the rhythm, mood and arrangement are completely different, thereby creating a completely new tune.

Trivia: Under Wraps was the first Jethro Tull album to be issued on CD. The album reached a respectable #18 in the UK but sales in the US were very poor—it topped at #76.

Verdict: A courageous and engaging album. 3/5

Shortly after recording the album, Jethro Tull reunited with David Palmer, who had written the theme song for a BBC television series entitled *The Blood Of The British*. The piece was a haunting tune with Gaelic lyrics called 'Coronach' and Jethro Tull did a beautiful job recording it. The single was released only in the UK in 1986.

The band also worked on another rather interesting side project for Palmer.

A Classic Case:
The London Symphony Orchestra Plays
The Music Of Jethro Tull

Released: UK: June 1993; US: December 1985

Track List: Locomotive Breath; Thick As A Brick; Elegy (Palmer); Bourée (J. S. Bach); Fly By Night (Anderson/Vettese); Aqualung (I. Anderson/J. Anderson); Too Old To Rock 'N' Roll—Too Young To Die; Medley: Teacher/Bungle In The Jungle/Rainbow Blues/Locomotive Breath; Living In The Past; WarChild. (All songs by Ian Anderson except where indicated; arranged by David Palmer.)

Cover Art: Designed by Ariola-Eurodisc/Studios J. Schlogl; photograph by Manfred Vormstein. The cover depicts the floor of a wine cellar, where an open box of 'Tull' wine sits beside a flute.

Personnel: The London Symphony Orchestra, conducted by David Palmer; Ian Anderson (flute); Martin Barre (electric guitar); Dave Pegg (bass); Peter-John Vettese (keyboards); Paul Burgess (drums). Produced by David Palmer.

Recording History: Before the release of *Under Wraps*, the band collaborated with David Palmer again on orchestral versions of Jethro Tull songs performed by the London Symphony Orchestra. Anderson, Barre, Pegg, Vettese and drummer Paul Burgess played on the record with the orchestra. It was recorded in the summer of 1984 and was first released in 1985. With *A Classic Case*, Palmer began a series of orchestrated rock albums; bands covered in subsequent years include Pink Floyd and Genesis.

Comments: An interesting experiment and certainly not the disaster it might have been. But whenever an orchestra attempts to rearrange and perform rock music, the results are always strange. The album is a hit and miss affair, with the best tracks being the ones that would ordinarily lend themselves to being orchestrated—'Bourée,' 'Fly By Night' and, believe it or not, 'WarChild.' The ones that make you wince are the rockers, like 'Aqualung' and 'Locomotive Breath.' On the positive side, I remember playing it for my dad and saying, "It's Jethro Tull's new album." He was impressed!

Trivia: It's not really a Jethro Tull album and probably shouldn't be listed as such. However, they *do* play on it and the music contained on it *is* Jethro Tull music. I'll leave it up to you whether or not it should be counted. The album was first released in Germany, of all places and then in the US on the RCA Red Seal 'classical' label. Oddly, it wasn't released in the UK until 1993. UK chart information doesn't exist, but it broke the US 100 and landed at #93.

Verdict: An oddity but worth a listen or two. 2/5

A new drummer was needed for the *Under Wraps* tour because Gerry Conway was still out of the picture. American Doane Perry (born 16 June 1956) successfully auditioned and was hired as a 'swing-shift' drummer. Relations with Conway were still good and the two drummers would share duties with the band for the next several years, depending on who was available.

While on tour in America in the fall of 1984, Ian Anderson developed laryngitis and was forced to cancel a couple of shows. The *Under Wraps* songs were terribly hard on his voice and he had to strain to carry through to the end on any given night. Ultimately, the condition grew worse and he began to experience throat spasms. Many of the shows scheduled in Australia had to be cancelled.

Back home in England, doctors advised Anderson to take a year off from singing—in the studio or on stage—in order to rest his voice. This hiatus ended up being two years, after which Ian Anderson's voice was sadly never the same. The rich timbre of his baritone singing voice was simply gone. On studio recordings he could get by just fine—it wasn't as if the voice was unrecognisable as Ian Anderson's, it was just tonally lower and softer in strength. On stage, however, it became increasingly problematic.

Anderson felt well enough to begin touring again in the summer of 1986. With Barre, Pegg, Vettese and Perry as the line-up, the band performed at some summer festivals and travelled to Israel and Hungary for the first time. The voice problems continued, however, and Anderson and the band were forced to transpose the keys of many classic songs to a lower register so that Anderson could sing them. Even so, Anderson often had to 'speak sing' to deliver some songs in performance. It wasn't ideal, but it worked. (Many fans and critics claimed that Anderson sounded a lot like Mark Knopfler of Dire Straits.)

Around this time, Terry Ellis sold his share of Chrysalis to Chris Wright and left the company. Jethro Tull's relationship with the label was tenuous, at best, because Chrysalis now seemed to focus their promotional efforts on newer, younger bands.

In the spring of 1987 the band went into the studio to record their next LP, something that would be considered a 'comeback' album.

Crest Of A Knave

Released: September 1987

Track List: Steel Monkey; Farm On The Freeway; Jump Start; Said She Was A Dancer; Dogs In The Midwinter [CD and cassette only]; Budapest; Mountain Men; The Waking Edge [CD and cassette only]; Raising Steam. (All songs by Ian Anderson.)

Cover Art: Calligraphy and heraldry by Andrew Jamieson, art direction by John Pasche. The single sleeve cover is simple and tasteful, featuring a Jethro Tull 'coat of arms.'

Personnel: Ian Anderson (vocals, flute, acoustic guitar, keyboards, synthesiser, drum programming, percussion); Martin Barre (electric and acoustic guitars); Dave Pegg (bass guitar, acoustic bass). With guests: Doane Perry (drums, percussion); Gerry Conway (drums, percussion); Ric Sanders (violin). Produced by Ian Anderson. Recording engineers: Ian Anderson, Martin Barre, Dave Pegg, Robin Black, Tim Matyear.

Recording Background: A permanent drummer had not yet been officially inducted into the band, so both Doane Perry and Gerry Conway contributed to various tracks on the album. Drum programming features on many tracks as well. Whether it was intentional or not, *Crest Of A Knave* reverts to the early 70s hard rock sound of, say, *Benefit* or

Aqualung, with heavy emphasis on electric guitar and flute. While the tradition of splicing in some quieter, acoustic moments continued, it is very much a hard rock album. The song 'Budapest' was inspired by the band's trip to Hungary. 'Farm On The Freeway' was no doubt inspired by Anderson's own experiences running salmon farms.

Comments: The album received the most FM airplay since *Aqualung*. Anderson's new vocal quality comes as a bit of a shock but he turns it into his advantage on studio recordings with a good mix that puts the voice front and centre and with a dramatic delivery that evokes wisdom and experience. Beyond that, the LP really cooks. The opening number 'Steel Monkey' is a driving, hard rock song that is sure to cause your upper body to bop in time. 'Farm On The Freeway' is a classic Anderson composition, moving from haunting verses to a heavy-metal instrumental middle that brings down the house. 'Jump Start' is another rocker that grooves along, building its dynamics with finesse. As far as I'm concerned, these three songs carry the album. The rest of the LP is all right, certainly not bad. 'Budapest' goes on a bit too long, but it's an epic piece of work. 'The Waking Edge' and 'Mountain Men' are forgettable. Still, *Crest Of A Knave* must be admired for its obvious professionalism, production quality and sheer energy.

Trivia: Everyone knows by now that Jethro Tull surprised the music industry by winning the Grammy for 'Hard Rock/Heavy Metal Performance' for *Crest Of A Knave*. Anderson justified the win by claiming that Jethro Tull did indeed play hard rock—it's just that it's hard rock with mandolins! The album made it to #19 in the UK and to #32 in the US.

Verdict: I love about half the album. It's not surprising, though, that the public would respond favourably to it, given the fact that it sounds more like the 'old' Jethro Tull. 3/5

To augment the band on keyboards for the tour, Don Airey was hired as a temporary stand-in, with Doane Perry sitting at the drum kit. The *Crest Of A Knave* tour was the most successful Tull tour in years. Of particular note was that in many venues the supporting act was the newly reformed Fairport Convention, Dave Pegg's old band. A man wearing many hats, Pegg performed with both Fairport and Tull each night!

During the tour, the band developed a relationship with Fairport Convention's guitarist and bouzouki player, Martin Allcock (born 5

January 1957). Fortunately, he could play keyboards, so he was asked to join Tull as keyboard player beginning in 1988.

20 Years Of Jethro Tull (Box Set)

Released: UK: June 1988; US: July 1988

Track List: 'The Radio Archives And Rare Tracks': A Song For Jeffrey; Love Story; Fat Man; Bourée (J. S. Bach); Stormy Monday Blues (Ecstine/Crowder/Hines); A New Day Yesterday; Cold Wind To Valhalla; Minstrel In The Gallery; Velvet Green; Grace; Jack Frost And The Hooded Crow; I'm Your Gun; Down At The End Of Your Road; Coronach (Palmer); Summerday Sands; Too Many Too; March, The Mad Scientist; Pan Dance; Strip Cartoon; King Henry's Madrigal (traditional, arr. Palmer); A Stitch In Time; 17; One For John Gee (Abrahams); Aeroplane (Anderson/Bernard); Sunshine Day (Abrahams). 'Flawed Gems And The Other Sides Of Tull': Lick Your Fingers Clean; The Chateau D'Isaster Tapes—a. Scenario, b. Audition, c. No Rehearsal; Beltane; Crossword; Saturation; Jack-A-Lynn; Motoreyes; Blues Instrumental (Untitled); Rhythm in Gold; Part Of The Machine; Mayhem, Maybe; Overhang; Kelpie; Living In These Hard Times; Under Wraps #2; Only Solitaire; Salamander; Moths; Nursie. 'The Essential Tull': The Witch's Promise; Bungle In The Jungle; Farm On The Freeway; Thick As A Brick; Sweet Dream; Clasp; Pibroch/Black Satin Dancer; Fallen On Hard Times; Cheap Day Return; Wond'ring Aloud; Dun Ringill; Life Is A Long Song; One White Duck/0^{10} = Nothing At All; Songs From The Wood; Living In The Past; Teacher (version #1); Aqualung (I. Anderson/J. Anderson); Locomotive Breath. (All songs by Ian Anderson except where indicated.)

Note: The box set was a limited edition release. The 'standard' edition is a single CD or double LP that omitted many of the tracks.

Cover Art: A set of 5 LPs, 3 cassettes, or 3 CDs, the package was presented in an LP-sized box with a silhouette of Ian Anderson standing on one leg and playing the flute on the cover. Along the edges of the cover are photographs of various Tull line-ups through the years. Included in the box is a booklet written by *A New Day* editors David Rees and Martin Webb that expertly chronicles the band's history.

Personnel: Being a retrospective collection, all of the Jethro Tull line-ups from 1968 to 1988 are represented. The 1988 incarnation, which recorded the song 'Part Of The Machine' was: Ian Anderson (vocals, flute, acoustic guitar); Martin Barre (electric and acoustic guitar); Dave Pegg (bass guitar); Martin Allcock (electric guitar, bouzouki, keyboards); Gerry Conway (drums, percussion).

Recording Background: Chrysalis Records wanted to do something special for Jethro Tull's 20th anniversary, so they enlisted the help of David Rees and Martin Webb, the editors of the Tull fanzine *A New Day*. The pair made recommendations of what rare tracks to include and wrote the liner notes for the box set booklet. Ian Anderson was reluctant to get involved with any kind of nostalgia project but once he got his feet wet he couldn't tear himself away. He spent a lot of time with recording engineers remastering and even overdubbing some instruments here and there to finish some of the unreleased stuff. The result was an amazing collection of familiar, rare, live and unreleased material from the Jethro Tull archives. About 65% was previously unavailable, which made the set a must-have for any serious fan. The album is divided into five categories. 'The Radio Archives' includes BBC performances such as those on *Top Gear*. 'The Rare Tracks' are made up of rare singles and B-sides, such as the 'Sunshine Day'/'Aeroplane' single, 'Coronach'/'Jack Frost And The Hooded Crow,' 'One For John Gee' and others. 'Flawed Gems' are unreleased tracks that for some reason or another were never included on the albums for which they had been originally meant. This includes three tracks from the aborted 1972 'Chateau D'Isaster Tapes.' 'The Other Sides Of Tull' is made up of unreleased and previously released tracks that happen to be some of Ian Anderson's personal favourites, mostly of the quiet, acoustic variety. And finally, 'The Essential Tull' consists of classics, either remastered studio versions or performed live in concert.

Comments: *20 Years Of Jethro Tull* set new standards for boxed retrospectives. The care that went into track selection shows because quite a few of the rare tracks that fans have clamoured for are included. The unreleased material includes many of the songs recorded in 1981 that never made it onto *The Broadsword And The Beast* LP. Nothing is wasted and it's a pure delight. Note that the casual/curious fan might not be too enthralled with the box because it's heavy on rare and unreleased material rather than on 'greatest hits.' Nevertheless, try to find the complete box set, for the abridged single CD version simply doesn't do justice to the magnificent collection that was assembled.

Trivia: The box set reached #78 in the UK and #97 in the US. While these numbers seem poor, it should be noted that it is rare for expensive box sets to break the top 100.

Verdict: A great collection and a must-have. 5/5

Jethro Tull went on tour again to promote the 20th anniversary. A wonderful gag was utilised at the shows: a nurse wheeled Ian Anderson onto the stage in a wheelchair and as the music began, he leapt out of the chair and assumed the familiar posturing! A banner at the back of the stage proclaimed, 'Oh No! Not Another Twenty Years of Jethro Tull!'

Rock Island

Released: UK: August 1989; US: September 1989

Track List: Kissing Willie; The Rattlesnake Trail; Ears Of Tin; Undressed To Kill; Rock Island; Heavy Water; Another Christmas Song; The Whaler's Dues; Big Riff And Mando; Strange Avenues. (All songs by Ian Anderson.)

Cover Art: The single sleeve illustrations were by Anton Morris and Jim Gibson. The front cover depicts the view of the ocean from a ship's porthole. A fist clutching a flute breaks the surface of the water.

Personnel: Ian Anderson (vocals, flute, acoustic guitar, mandolin, keyboards, drums); Martin Barre (electric guitar); Dave Pegg (bass guitar, mandolin); Doane Perry (drums, percussion). With guests: Martin Allcock (keyboards); Peter-John Vettese (keyboards). Produced and engineered by Ian Anderson.

Recording Background: The album was recorded during spring 1989 at Ian Anderson's and Dave Pegg's home studios. The intention was clearly to capitalise on the Grammy winning 'hard rock/heavy metal' *Crest Of A Knave* and it is in that direction that the new album goes. Nearly every song is a rocker with blistering guitar at the forefront. Martin Allcock and Peter-John Vettese shared duties on keyboards, but it was Allcock who went on tour to support the album.

Comments: The creativity and enthusiasm that was present on *Crest Of A Knave* is missing from *Rock Island.* Despite three excellent songs, the dynamic 'Ears Of Tin' and 'Rock Island' and the sequel to the 1968 B-side, 'Another Christmas Song,' the album tends to rock along at the same level throughout. 'Kissing Willie,' a UK only single, is amusing but ultimately unmemorable and the same could be said for the rest of the numbers. The old Ian Anderson cynicism is back and, combined with the ragged vocals, it creates a presence that is uncomfortably intimidating.

Trivia: The album scored a high #18 in the UK and #56 in the US.

Verdict: It rocks, but these guys can do much better. 2/5

Another album, another tour. The *Rock Island* shows were another success, catering to the hard rock enthusiasts who had 'discovered' Jethro Tull with *Crest Of A Knave*. The band continued to tour into 1990, after which, aside from a few gigs in 1991, Martin Allcock called it a day and chose to keep his activities relegated to Fairport Convention.

Live At The Hammersmith '84—The Friday Rock Show Sessions

Released: December 1990 (UK only)

Track List: Locomotive Breath (instrumental); Hunting Girl; Under Wraps #1; Later, That Same Evening (Anderson/Vettese); Pussy Willow; Living In The Past; Locomotive Breath; Too Old To Rock 'N' Roll—Too Young To Die. (All songs by Ian Anderson except where indicated.)

Cover Art: As this is an unofficial album not released by Chrysalis, the artwork is not up to the usual standards. The cover is a collage of comic book characters in various stages of emoting. The Jethro Tull logo from the Under Wraps tour sits in the centre.

Personnel: Ian Anderson (vocals, flute, acoustic guitar); Martin Barre (electric guitar); Dave Pegg (bass guitar, mandolin); Peter-John Vettese (keyboards); Doane Perry (drums, percussion). Produced by Tony Wilson and Dale Griffin. Recording engineer: Dave Dade.

Recording Background: The BBC originally broadcast this material on 27 December 1984, live from the Hammersmith Odeon in London. Raw Fruit Records asked for permission to release it and Ian Anderson gave his blessing.

Comments: It's a bit jarring to hear an excerpt from the Under Wraps tour six years later, but what the heck... Unfortunately, the sound quality is not very good, much like a fairly decent bootleg. It's a poor representation of Jethro Tull in concert.

Trivia: This was the first Jethro Tull release outside of Chrysalis Records. There is no chart placing information because its distribution was limited.

Verdict: For completists only. 1/5

6: The Legend Lives On (1991 – 2002)

Catfish Rising

Released: September 1991

Track List: This Is Not Love; Occasional Demons; Roll Yer Own; Rocks On The Road; Sparrow On The Schoolyard Wall; Thinking Round Corners; Still Loving You Tonight; Doctor To My Disease; Like A Tall Thin Girl; White Innocence; Sleeping With The Dog; Gold-Tipped Boots, Black Jacket And Tie; When Jesus Came To Play. (All songs by Ian Anderson.)

Cover Art: Designed by Phil Rogers and John Pasche, illustration by Jim Gibson, monogram and logo by Geoff Halpin. With CDs now the standard medium, the days of extravagant album covers were long gone. The cover for the new album is a simple and tasteful abstract illustration of a catfish jumping out of water.

Personnel: Ian Anderson (vocals, flute, acoustic and electric guitars, acoustic and electric mandolins, keyboards, drums); Martin Barre (electric guitar); Dave Pegg (bass guitar); Doane Perry (drums, percussion). With guests: Andy Giddings (keyboards); John 'Rabbit' Bundrick (keyboards); Foss Paterson (keyboards); Matthew Pegg (bass guitar). Produced by Ian Anderson, engineered by Ian Anderson and Tim Matyear, assisted by Mark Tucker.

Recording Background: Recorded in the winter and spring of 1991, *Catfish Rising* is a 'return to roots.' The album take on a blues or folk-oriented style, has less hard rock than recent albums and focuses on poetic lyrics and guitar work. With a permanent keyboard player not yet in place, several session musicians worked on the album and contributed separately to various numbers. Dave Pegg's son Matthew also performed on some of the sessions when Dave was unavailable. Several songs were ultimately not included on the album and held back for later release as B-sides. 'This Is Not Love' was released as a CD single with the non-album bonus tracks 'Night In The Wilderness' and a live rendition of 'Jump Start.'

Comments: Some fans complained that *Catfish Rising* was a step backward. I heartily disagree. It's a wonderful, light-hearted, accessible album that stands as one of Jethro Tull's better works. It is full of wit and wisdom—certainly what you'd expect from Ian Anderson—but it's more than what we've had in a long time. Not every song is a classic, but there are some great ones. The obligatory hard rocker, 'This Is Not Love,' is okay, but the album really gets into a groove beginning with the third track, 'Roll Yer Own.' This number is a finger-snapper and sets the pace for the remainder of the LP. 'Thinking Round Corners' is a mini-masterpiece that sounds more like something Captain Beefheart might have done—it is full of surreal imagery and nonsensical musical shifts. 'Still Loving You Tonight' is a soulful love song, a rarity for Tull. 'White Innocence,' the longest piece on the album, is a highlight that recalls the 'Baker St. Muse' days. Guitars and mandolins dominate the album and suffice it to say that the musicianship is superb.

Trivia: The album made it to #27 in the UK but only to #88 in the US.

Verdict: A great way to start the new decade! 4/5

It seemed as if Jethro Tull toured non-stop in the 90s, but there were to be a few more personnel changes. Andy Giddings (born 10 July 1963) apparently made a good impression at the *Catfish Rising* sessions. He was asked to become Jethro Tull's permanent keyboard player. Doane Perry, however, had some outside commitments for a few months, so another Fairport Convention alumnus, Dave Mattacks, was asked to sit in for him. Mattacks had three decades of experience and fit in well with the team. This line-up toured until March 1992. That month, Chrysalis released a UK-only double CD single, *Rocks On The Road*. It was a fine set with a fair amount of music on it, nearly enough for a full album. It contained the LP version of 'Rocks On The Road,' some home demos of other songs and live performances.

In April, it was decided to take advantage of the trend in 'unplugged' concerts. Anderson temporarily pared down the band to a quartet—himself, Barre, Pegg and Mattacks—and went on a semi-acoustic tour entitled A Little Light Music. It wasn't totally 'unplugged'; some numbers, such as 'Aqualung' or 'Locomotive Breath,' had to be performed with electric guitars and drum-bashing, so eventually the name of the tour was changed to The Light And Dark Tour to avoid confusion!

A Little Light Music

Released: September 1992

Track List: Someday The Sun Won't Shine For You; Living In The Past; Life Is A Long Song; Under Wraps #2; Rocks On The Road; Nursie; Too Old To Rock 'N' Roll—Too Young To Die; One White Duck; A New Day Yesterday; John Barleycorn (traditional); Look Into The Sun; A Christmas Song; From A Dead Beat To An Old Greazer; This Is Not Love; Bourée (J. S. Bach); Pussy Willow; Locomotive Breath. (All songs by Ian Anderson except where indicated.)

Cover Art: Designed and illustrated by Bogdan Zarkowski. The attractive art deco cover features an abstract caricature of Ian Anderson wearing a top hat and tuxedo. Beneath him sit four identical abstract musicians, playing guitars.

Personnel: Ian Anderson (vocals, flute, acoustic guitar, mandolin); Martin Barre (electric and acoustic guitars); Dave Pegg (acoustic bass guitar, mandolin); Dave Mattacks (drums, percussion, keyboards). Produced by Ian Anderson, engineered by Leon Phillips.

Recording Background: Recorded at several live concerts during the A Little Light Music/Light And Dark Tour in the summer of 1992, the album is meant to be representative of the 'nearly unplugged' side of Jethro Tull. The tracks came from shows recorded in Germany, Switzerland, Austria, Czechoslovakia, Greece, Turkey and Israel.

Comments: This is a wonderful live album and a pleasure to listen to. Once again, my personal prejudices against live albums keep it from receiving a higher rating but I think if I were going to listen to any live album by Jethro Tull, this would be it. What really makes it special is the inclusion of rare gems that the band hadn't performed in years, such as 'From A Dead Beat To An Old Greazer,' 'Life Is A Long Song' and 'One White Duck.' Other highlights include 'Bourée' (with a new middle section that has not been recorded before), 'A New Day Yesterday' (with a lot of killer improvisation) and a newly arranged 'Living In The Past.' Ian Anderson's voice is okay but you can hear him straining at times.

Trivia: Greek musician George Dalaras joined Tull on-stage in Athens for a rendition of the traditional Celtic tune, 'John Barleycorn.' The Greek/Italian/Israeli editions of *A Little Light Music* feature the duet by Anderson and Dalaras but in the rest of the world Dalaras' vocals are erased from the track. The album reached #34 in the UK and a disappointing #150 in America.

Verdict: A gem of a live album. 3/5

At the end of 1992, Chrysalis made the decision to go all out for Jethro Tull's 25th anniversary in 1993. How could they outdo the 20th anniversary 3-CD box set released in 1988? By releasing a 4-CD box set, a 2-CD 'greatest hits' collection, several singles and a video! A further box set of unreleased live and studio tracks was planned for later in the year but this was cut down to a 2-CD set, *Nightcap*. The singles were various versions of 'Living In The Past': a 7' vinyl single of the original version backed with a song recorded in 1989, 'Hardliner'; a double CD single consisting of original and live versions of 'Living In The Past,' plus several *Catfish Rising* out-takes; and a 12' vinyl dance remix of 'Living In The Past.' Talk about nostalgia!

25th Anniversary Box Set

Released: April 1993

Track List: Disk One: 'Remixed': My Sunday Feeling; A Song For Jeffrey; Living In The Past; Teacher (version #2); Sweet Dream; Cross-Eyed Mary; The Witch's Promise; Life Is A Long Song; Bungle In The Jungle; Minstrel In The Gallery; Cold Wind To Valhalla; Too Old To Rock 'N' Roll—Too Young To Die; Songs From The Wood; Heavy Horses; Black Sunday; Broadsword. Disk Two: 'Live At Carnegie Hall, 1970': Nothing Is Easy; My God; With You There To Help Me; A Song For Jeffrey; To Cry You A Song?; Sossity—You're A Woman; Reasons For Waiting; We Used To Know; Guitar Solo (Barre); For A Thousand Mothers. 'The Beacons Bottom Tapes': So Much Trouble (McGhee); My Sunday Feeling; Someday The Sun Won't Shine For You; Living In The Past; Bourée (J. S. Bach); With You There To Help Me; Thick As A Brick; Cheerio; A New Day Yesterday; Protect And Survive; Jack-A-Lynn; The Whistler; My God; Aqualung (I. Anderson/ J. Anderson). 'Potpourri: Live Across The World And Through The Years': To Be Sad Is A Mad Way To Be; Back To The Family; A Passion Play Extract; Wind-Up/Locomotive Breath/Land Of Hope And Glory; Seal Driver; Nobody's Car (Anderson/Barre/Vettese); Pussy Willow; Budapest; Nothing Is Easy; Kissing Willie; Still Loving You Tonight; Beggar's Farm (Anderson/Abrahams); Passion Jig; A Song

For Jeffrey; Living In The Past. (All songs by Ian Anderson except where indicated.)

Cover Art: Package and sleeve design by Bogdan Zarkowski. A beautifully designed box set! The deceit is that it is a cigar box, with 'Jethro Tull—25th Anniversary' emblazoned on the top. Upon opening the box, one finds a booklet. On the cover of the booklet are what appear to be cigars—but on second glance, they're really wooden flutes! The four compact disks are contained neatly beneath the booklet, which is full of photos, trivia and essays all about our favourite rock band.

Personnel: As the box set is a retrospective, all Jethro Tull line-ups from 1968 to 1993 are represented. The 1993 band consisted of: Ian Anderson (vocals, flute, acoustic guitar, keyboards, percussion); Martin Barre (electric and acoustic guitars); Dave Pegg (bass guitar, mandolin, acoustic and electric guitars); Andy Giddings (keyboards); and Doane Perry (drums, percussion).

Recording Background: On the first disk of this classy box set, entitled 'Remixed,' classic Tull songs were remixed to create, at times, a completely different version. The second disk contained the famous Carnegie Hall concert from 1970, minus the two tracks that originally appeared on *Living In The Past* in 1972. The third disk is actually a brand new album, recorded in 1992 at Beacons Bottom studios with the new Tull line-up that included new member Andy Giddings on keyboards. There were no new songs recorded; the current band laid down completely new versions of old classics. The fourth disk was culled from live performances ranging from the years 1969 to 1991.

Comments: Despite the effort that went into making this box set better than the 1988 anniversary set, it doesn't quite do it. Still, it's an impressive collection of material and certainly a fan's delight. The 'Remixed' disk is a bit superfluous. Some of the remixed versions are interesting and different but was it really worth devoting an entire disk to this experiment? The live Carnegie Hall concert on disk two is worth the price of the box. It captures a very young Jethro Tull at its most vibrant and energetic. This material is a revelation. It's a great moment when Ian Anderson loses his breath at the end of 'My God' and has to take a few moments to regain it. Disk three, the newly recorded old songs, is a mixed bag. Some of them are quite good, such as 'My Sunday Feeling,' 'With You There To Help Me,' 'Bourée' and 'A New Day Yesterday.' Others are hampered by the sad fact that the older, more familiar versions sound better. The fourth disk of live material is very good, although there is no material from 1970 – 1974 and very little from the 70s at all. The two tracks from 1969 are excellent and the recent versions of 'Beggar's Farm' and 'Living In The Past' are super. The major Tull fan is really going to love the collection but again the casual fan that wants a 'greatest hits' set will be disappointed.

Trivia: Not all of the third disk was recorded at Beacons Bottom—five songs were recorded at Dave Pegg's or Martin Barre's home studios.

Verdict: Good fun and a pleasure, although at least a third of the set is unnecessary. 3/5

Nightcap—The Unreleased Masters, 1973 – 1991

Released: UK: November 1993; US: January 2000

Track List: 'My Round—The Chateau D'Isaster Tapes': First Post; Animelee; Tiger Toon; Look At The Animals; Law Of The Bungle; Law Of The Bungle, Part II; Left Right; Solitaire; Critique Oblique; Post Last; Scenario; Audition; No Rehearsal. 'Your Round—Unreleased And Rare Tracks': Paradise Steakhouse; Sea Lion II; Piece Of Cake; Quartet; Silver River Turning; Crew Nights; The Curse; Rosa On The Factory Floor; A Small Cigar; Man Of Principle; Commons Brawl; No Step; Drive On The Young Side Of Life; I Don't Want To Be Me; Broadford Bazaar; Lights Out; Truck Stop Runner; Hardliner. (All songs by Ian Anderson.)

Cover Art: Designed by Bogdan Zarkowski. The cover features a bottle of whiskey with the title information on the label. Simple and tasteful.

Personnel: Being a compilation of rare and unreleased material, all Jethro Tull line-ups between 1972 and 1991 are represented.

Recording Background: As part of the 25th anniversary celebration in 1993, this collection was originally scheduled to be another 4-CD box set. It was ultimately pared down to two CDs and only released in the UK. Ian Anderson stated that he never would have released any of the material had it not been for the great demand by the hard-core fans. The CD was heavily imported to the US; oddly, it wasn't released in America until 2000. The title has a mistake in it—'The Unreleased Masters, 1973 – 1991' should actually read '1972 – 1991' (the entire first disk, the legendary 'Chateau D'Isaster Tapes,' was recorded in

1972). Three of the tracks had been released on the *20 Years Of Jethro Tull* box set and 'Solitaire' was released as 'Only Solitaire' on *War-Child*; otherwise, the remainder of the songs was previously unavailable. The tracks on the second disk are from recordings ranging from 1974 to 1991. Several of these came from the well of tunes recorded in 1981 that weren't used on *The Broadsword And The Beast*. A few tracks had been issued as B-sides, such as 'Hardliner,' 'Man Of Principle,' 'Piece Of Cake,' 'Rosa On The Factory Floor,' 'Silver River Turning' and 'Truck Stop Runner.' The others were unreleased. Ian Anderson overdubbed flute and other instruments onto some tracks to complete and bring them up to date.

Comments: An underrated collection! The 'Chateau D'Isaster Tapes' is fascinating from an historical perspective. Given the fact that this material was recorded in between *Thick As A Brick* and *A Passion Play*, it's enlightening to hear another group of complex songs from that Progressive period. Much of the material was eventually reworked for *A Passion Play* and it's fun to spot the similarities. Granted, some of the 'Law Of The Bungle' stuff is silly but instrumentally the work is superb. The tracks on the second disk are a mixed bag but most of them are quite worthy of release. My favourites are 'Paradise Steakhouse,' 'Quartet,' 'Crew Nights,' 'The Curse,' 'Man Of Principle,' 'Commons Brawl' and 'I Don't Want To Be Me.' No classics but all good stuff.

Trivia: Anderson dictated that his songwriting royalties from the album go to charities, specifically the Balnain House, Home of Highland Music, Inverness, Scotland and to the Animal Health Trust.

Verdict: If you're a serious Tull fan, you're going to love it despite the few dodgy pieces. 3/5

The tours to celebrate the 25th anniversary kept Jethro Tull busy for the next two years! They went all over the world, entertaining old fans and developing new ones. Set lists included songs from the entire catalogue, even some that they hadn't performed since the original year of release. Unfortunately, Dave Pegg found himself increasingly busy with the creation of his own recording studio, record company and his commitments with Fairport Convention. Before the completion of Tull's next studio album in 1995, he would gracefully bow out of the band.

In 1994, Martin Barre released his first solo album (excluding a CD and cassette entitled *A Summer Band*, released in 1993 and sold only through the Tull fanzine, *A New Day*). Entitled *A Trick Of Memory*, it was released (but poorly distributed) by ZYX Music.

Also during 1994, Ian Anderson decided to take flute lessons! For over twenty-five years he had been playing it improperly, using wrong fingering and not utilising its full octave potential. While on a visit to India, he retaught himself how to play and the difference was immediately apparent. His new knowledge and ability would gain maximum exposure on his next two projects—a second Ian Anderson solo album and a new Jethro Tull LP.

EMI (which now owned Chrysalis) came to Anderson and suggested that he do a 'classical' album consisting of flute and orchestra. The result was an all-instrumental opus entitled *Divinities—12 Dances With God*, released on the EMI classical label (Angel in the US) in late spring of 1995. Anderson employed the multi-keyboard talents of Andy Giddings for the work and came up with a magnificent exploration of the world's religions. He even did an abbreviated tour for the album, billed simply as 'Ian Anderson'—although he brought along Giddings, Doane Perry, bass player Jonathan Noyce (who would soon become Dave Pegg's replacement) and violinist Chris Leslie. The entire *Divinities* album was performed in the first half of the concert. After an interval, 'orchestrated' versions of classic Jethro Tull songs were performed.

While this was going on, another 'unofficially official' live Tull album was released.

In Concert

Released: UK: April 1995; US: February 1996

Track List: Minstrel In The Gallery/Cross-Eyed Mary; This Is Not Love; Rocks On The Road; Heavy Horses; Like A Tall Thin Girl; Still Loving You Tonight; Thick As A Brick; A New Day Yesterday; Blues Jam; Jump Start. (All songs by Ian Anderson.)

Cover Art: Designed by Definition, the cover features a superb colour photograph of Ian Anderson and Martin Barre on stage.

Personnel: Ian Anderson (vocals, flute, acoustic guitar, mandolin, harmonica); Martin Barre (electric and acoustic guitars); Dave Pegg (bass guitar); Martin Allcock (keyboards); Doane Perry (drums, percussion). Produced by Pete Ritzema. Recording engineer: Mike Engels.

Recording Background: This was the second non-Chrysalis Jethro Tull release, a live performance recorded for the BBC at the Hammersmith Odeon, London, on 8 October 1991 during the *Catfish Rising* tour. Ian Anderson approved its release on the Windsong label in the UK and on Griffin Music in the US.

Comments: It's a much better BBC live album than 1990's *Live At The Hammersmith, 1984.* The sound quality is immensely improved and the performances are energetic and engaging. Unfortunately, Ian Anderson's voice exhibits the war-torn quality that has plagued him since 1984 but otherwise the musicianship is professional and polished.

Verdict: Not bad for a live album. 2/5

Roots To Branches

Released: September 1995

Track List: Roots To Branches; Rare And Precious Chain; Out Of The Noise; This Free Will; Valley; Dangerous Veils; Beside Myself; Wounded, Old And Treacherous; At Last, Forever; Stuck In The August Rain; Another Harry's Bar. (All songs by Ian Anderson)

Cover Art: Design/artwork by Bogdan Zarkowski. The album showcases an understated piece of art illustrating the 'circle of life'—tree roots around the outside edge grow toward the centre into branches and leaves; a sun with a face sits in the middle.

Personnel: Ian Anderson (vocals, flutes, acoustic guitar); Martin Barre (electric guitar); Andy Giddings (keyboards); Doane Perry (drums, percussion); Dave Pegg (bass guitar). With guest Steve Bailey (bass guitar). Produced and engineered by Ian Anderson.

Recording Background: Produced more or less simultaneously with Ian Anderson's second solo album, *Roots To Branches* marked another transition for Jethro Tull. The album was recorded at Anderson's home studio off and on between December 1994 and June 1995. Dave Pegg played on only three tracks before leaving the band. Session man Steve Bailey played on the remaining songs. Anderson's recent trip to India had a great influence on both the solo album and the new Tull LP. The music contains a great deal of exotic Eastern flavour, achieved partly by Anderson playing wooden and bamboo flutes along with the standard concert flute. The songs deal with the thematic concepts of life, death, tolerance and free will, coloured by the familiar Ian Anderson cynicism.

Comments: Yet another controversial album among fans, *Roots To Branches* is a complex, ambitious and meaningful work that beckons to be explored with repeated listenings. At the same time it is highly accessible, containing memorable melodies and hooks. I believe it's the strongest Jethro Tull studio album since *Songs From The Wood*! There is not a weak song on the entire thing and the musicianship is the best it's ever been. Anderson's flute playing is simply magnificent and is a highlight of the album. The lyrics are compelling, mysterious and thought provoking. 'Haunting' is a good word to describe the album. Every song is great but my favourites would have to be: 'Roots To Branches' with its unpredictable changes in tempo and musical styles; 'Rare And Precious Chain' with its droning, sitar-like guitar work; 'Valley' with its outstanding lyrics that tell an epic allegory about conformity; 'Beside Myself,' an immediate Tull classic that recalls the older dynamic pieces such as 'My God'; and 'Wounded, Old And Treacherous,' with its Zappa-like feel and clever message. *Roots To Branches* is a mature work boiling over with intelligence, a fulfilment of the promise of genius made so many years ago with works like *Thick As A Brick*.

Trivia: Roots To Branches was the last Jethro Tull album released by Chrysalis Records. The album reached #20 in the UK and, sadly, only #114 in the US.

Verdict: One of the very best Jethro Tull albums. Deep, accessible and brilliant. 5/5

Jonathan Noyce (born 15 July 1971) became the youngest member ever to join Jethro Tull when he was permanently hired as bass player for the *Roots To Branches* tour.

Jethro Tull took the show to South America in the spring of 1996, where, in March, Ian Anderson injured his left knee on a poor stage in Lima, Peru. Anderson finished the show in a chair and continued the tour performing from a wheelchair. Not wishing to cancel concerts in Australia and New Zealand, Anderson forged ahead, knee or no knee and took the band to the other side of the world in May. But after four shows, he was in tremendous pain and had to stop. Rushed to the hospital, he learned that he had a potentially deadly blood clot (thrombosis) in his leg. The rest of the tour was cancelled while Anderson was forced to stay in bed.

Anderson spent the summer recovering but insisted on honouring tour commitments for the fall. By September, the band was back in America, this time touring with support act Emerson, Lake and Palmer.

Anderson was able to stand and move around the stage but a park bench was provided for him, where he could sit and rest when he needed to.

A Jethro Tull tribute album was released in 1996. Entitled *To Cry You A Song—A Collection Of Tull Tales*, the CD featured various artists performing covers of Jethro Tull songs and was released on Magna Carta Records. What made it particularly interesting was that former Tull members—namely Mick Abrahams, Clive Bunker, Glenn Cornick and Dave Pegg—all made contributions. Martin Barre also released a second solo album, *The Meeting*, on the Presshouse/Imago labels.

Jethro Tull continued to tour through 1997, 1998 and 1999. Ian Anderson turned fifty in 1998 and began to work on a third solo album. By early 1999, *The Secret Language Of Birds* was completed, but it was held back for another year so that things could get worked out with a new record label. Tull's contract with Chrysalis/EMI had expired in the fall of 1998 and both parties declined to renew it. In May of 1999, Anderson signed a new contract with Fuel 2000 (North America) and Papillon Records (Europe and rest of the world). Jethro Tull was the first band signed by the new companies, so it was sensible that the first release be a proper Jethro Tull album of new material rather than Anderson's solo LP.

J-Tull Dot Com

Released: August 1999

Track List: Spiral; Dot Com; AWOL; Nothing @ All (Giddings); Wicked Windows; Hunt By Numbers; Hot Mango Flush (Anderson/ Barre); El Niño; Black Mamba; Mango Surprise; Bends Like A Willow; Far Alaska; The Dog Ear Years; A Gift Of Roses; bonus track—The Secret Language Of Birds. (All songs by Ian Anderson except where indicated.)

Cover Art: Painting by Ian Anderson, based on a sculpture by Michael Cooper; designed by Bogdan Zarkowski. The cover is a painting of a garden statue, Amun, holding a bowl of fire. For the US market, the statue's genitals are painted out but they are left intact for the rest of the world!

Personnel: Ian Anderson (vocals, concert flute, bamboo flute, bouzouki, acoustic guitar); Martin Barre (electric and acoustic guitars); Andy Giddings (Hammond organ, piano, accordion, chromatic and qwerty keyboards); Doane Perry (drums, percussion); Jonathan Noyce (bass guitar). With guest Najma Akhtar (backing vocals). Produced by Ian Anderson. Engineered by Ian Anderson, assisted by Martin Barre, Doane Perry, Andy Giddings, Jonathan Noyce and Tim Matyear.

Recording Background: After several years of intense touring, ill health and recording a third solo album, Ian Anderson brought the band back into his home studio in early 1999 to make the last Jethro Tull album of the 20th Century. Now with a new label, the intention was clearly to make something commercial and accessible to not only please the hard-core fans but also the general CD-buying public. The group of songs on *J-Tull Dot Com* (the title was a clever way to promote Tull's new official website) covered a variety of subjects, such as romance, bad weather, snakes, the hunting behaviour of cats and ageing.

Comments: A fine album, nothing terribly brilliant but also nothing particularly weak. It's a good, middle-tier album that strikes a balance between what is expected from Jethro Tull and experimentation. 'Dot Com' (also released as a single) is an Eastern-influenced, lovely song augmented by female vocalist Najma Akhtar. 'A Gift Of Roses' is perhaps the most traditionally Tull-like song, recalling tunes like 'Life Is A Long Song.' 'Far Alaska' moves along with an infectious beat and 'The Dog Ear Years' is an amusing and affectionate look at turning fifty years old. 'Hot Mango Flush' and its reprise, 'Mango Surprise,' are odd Caribbean-influenced novelties that make you shake your head and smile in bewilderment. Two or three tracks tend to go on too long and don't provide enough variety but overall the LP is a solid effort.

Trivia: The first Jethro Tull album on the new label, Fuel 2000/Papillon. UK chart position reached #44 and in the US #161.

Verdict: A pleasant, enjoyable album. 3/5

Of course, Jethro Tull went on tour to promote the new album as soon as it was in the stores. Ian Anderson released *The Secret Language Of Birds* in March 2000 and kept the band on tour for the next two years.

In January 2002, the original 1968 line-up of Anderson, Mick Abrahams, Glenn Cornick and Clive Bunker got together in a British blues club and performed and recorded three songs: 'A Song For Jeffrey,' 'My Sunday Feeling' and 'Someday The Sun Won't Shine For You.' About the reunion, Anderson had this to say: "Interesting experience. They had done their homework so we just had one rehearsal of each song. We are all older, fatter and balder but the same basic chemistry was there and judging by the DVD we had a good time!"

A little later in the spring, the first Jethro Tull performance DVD was released (including clips from the original line-up reunion), along with an accompanying audio CD.

Living With The Past

Released: April 2002

Track List: Intro; My Sunday Feeling; Roots To Branches; Jack In The Green; The Habanero Reel; Sweet Dream; In The Grip Of Stronger Stuff; Aqualung (I. Anderson/J. Anderson); Locomotive Breath; Living In The Past; Protect and Survive; Nothing Is Easy; Wond'ring Aloud; Life Is A Long Song; A Christmas Song; Cheap Day Return; Mother Goose; Dot Com; Fat Man; Someday The Sun Won't Shine For You; Cheerio. (All songs by Ian Anderson except where indicated.)

Cover Art: Designed by Bogdan Zarkowski. The tasteful and attractive CD cover features a stained-glass window with a silhouette of Ian Anderson, playing the flute and standing on one leg. Clouds and a blue sky fill the silhouette.

Personnel: Ian Anderson (vocals, concert flute, bamboo flute, acoustic guitar, harmonica, mandolin); Martin Barre (electric and acoustic guitars, flute); Andy Giddings (keyboards, accordion); Doane Perry (drums, percussion); Jonathan Noyce (bass guitar). With guests Mick Abrahams (vocals, electric and acoustic guitars), Clive Bunker (drums) and Glenn Cornick (bass guitar) on track 20, Dave Pegg (bass guitar, mandolin) on tracks 15, 16 and 17, James Duncan (drums) on track 14, Brian Thomas, Justine Tomlinson, Malcolm Henderson, Juliet Tomlinson (violins, viola, cello) on tracks 13 and 14. Produced and mixed by Ian Anderson.

Recording Background: The album consists of live performances recorded at various times. The first eleven tracks and final one are from a concert at the Hammersmith in the UK in 2001. Track 12 is from a Paris concert in 1999. Tracks 13 and 14 were recorded in January 2002 in a 'Stately Home Session.' Tracks 15, 16 and 17 were recorded in a dressing room backstage in Zurich in 1989 (these tracks were originally released on a promotional CD single that same year). Tracks 18 and 19 are from a 2 Meter TV session in Holland, 1999. Finally, track 20 is from the reunion of the original 1968 Tull line-up on 29 January 2002.

Comments: An excellent live album, beautifully recorded and produced. The sound is terrific and Anderson's voice sounds full and strong. All of the songs from the Hammersmith show are perhaps the best recorded live performances by Jethro Tull available to the public to date. These, plus the Paris concert track, make up the more 'electric' set on the CD, while the latter nine tracks comprise a more or less acoustic set.

Trivia: The reunion of the original 1968 line-up took place at Kelly's Bar in Leamington Spa, in the midlands of England. Ian Anderson's son James co-engineered the album.

Verdict: A better than usual live album. 4/5

As the band's 35th anniversary approaches, it's clear that Jethro Tull doesn't give up. Still recording and touring into the new millennium, they continue to entertain millions. To date Jethro Tull has sold over sixty million albums worldwide. The number of concerts approaches the 3,000 mark. The band consistently sells out medium-sized venues. "We try to target theatres with 1500 to 2000 seats," says Anderson. "Every tour usually includes a sports arena or two, some large outdoor festival-type places and we do very well. I don't like clubs—that's a little too intimate and up-close for my taste, especially if people are drinking and *especially* if people are smoking. Perhaps if it's an acoustic show, that might be different."

After an extensive tour in 2002, Ian Anderson plans to release a fourth solo album, do an acoustic tour and perhaps work on a project involving orchestral arrangements of Jethro Tull music or his own original stuff. He certainly has no plans to slow down.

Jethro Tull has indeed proven that you're never too old to rock 'n' roll and most definitely too young to die.

7: The Solo Albums, The Compilations, Singles And Videos

The discussion of Jethro Tull solo albums in this book is confined to releases by band members who are currently or were in Jethro Tull at the time of the specific album's release. Many former band members have released albums as solo artists or with other bands. For a more in-depth discography by ex-Tullers, Greg Russo's *Flying Colours—The Jethro Tull Reference Manual* is an excellent resource.

Ian Anderson Solo Albums

Ian Anderson has released three solo albums, with a fourth due November 2002 or thereabouts.

Walk Into Light

Released: UK: November 1983; US: December 1983

Track List: Fly By Night (Anderson/Vettese); Made In England (Anderson/Vettese); Walk Into Light; Trains (Anderson/Vettese); End Game; Black And White Television; Toad In The Hole; Looking For Eden; User-Friendly (Anderson/Vettese); Different Germany (Anderson/Vettese). (All songs by Ian Anderson except where indicated.)

Cover Art: Conceived by Ian Anderson, art direction by John Pasche, photography by Martyn Goddard. The simple, single sleeve cover features a black and white photo of Ian Anderson (looking clean-cut with short hair and a neatly trimmed beard). In an unusual move, the track titles are listed on the cover.

Personnel: Ian Anderson (vocals, flute, acoustic, electric and bass guitars, drum programming); Peter-John Vettese (piano, synthesisers, backing vocals). Produced and engineered by Ian Anderson.

Recording Background: Ian Anderson's first solo album was recorded during spring and summer of 1983. He chose to enlist the services of current Tull keyboard player Peter-John Vettese; he and Vettese are the only two musicians who appear on the LP. Working against the expectations for a flute and acoustic guitar-driven collection of songs, Anderson instead surprised his fans by delivering a technology-driven LP full of synthesisers, drum programming and the occasional flute. In another unusual move, Anderson shared songwriting credit with Vettese on half the songs.

Comments: Walk Into Light is a solid album with several very good songs. Even though the technological aspects dominate the LP, it's easily recognisable as Ian Anderson (although you're most likely to think it's Jethro Tull with a more modern sound). At any rate, the album is very 80s, a clear product of its time. Fans tended to stay away from it because of its unorthodox approach to Tull music. That said, I feel it's an underrated album. The best songs are quite memorable and they carry the LP: 'Fly By Night,' 'Made In England,' 'Walk Into Light,' 'Looking For Eden' and 'Different Germany.'

Trivia: In the UK the album reached #78.

Verdict: It's no classic, but it's an enjoyable record. Anderson is to be credited for taking a courageous step forward in experimenting with new technology as a dry run for the next Tull album. 3/5

Divinities—12 Dances With God

Released: UK: April 1995; US: May 1995

Track List: In A Stone Circle; In Sight Of The Minaret; In A Black Box; In The Grip Of Stronger Stuff; In Maternal Grace; In The Money-lender's Temple; In Defence Of Faiths; At Their Father's Knee; En Afrique; In The Olive Garden; In The Pay Of Spain; In The Times Of India (Bombay Valentine). (All songs by Ian Anderson; additional material by Andrew Giddings. Orchestrations by Ian Anderson and Andrew Giddings.)

Cover Art: Designed by Bogdan Zarkowski. The single sleeve album sports a beautiful abstract painting that captures the mystical aspects of the music, giving a symbolic nod to four great religions—Christianity, Judaism, Hinduism and Islam. Shiva dances in the centre of the picture.

Personnel: Ian Anderson (concert and alto flute, bamboo flute, other wooden flutes and whistles); Andrew Giddings (keyboards, orchestral tones and colours). With guests: Doane Perry (percussion); Douglas Mitchell (clarinet); Christopher Cowie (oboe); Jonathon Carrey (violin); Nina Greslin (cello); Randy Wigs (harp); Sid Gander (French horn); Dan Redding (trumpet). Produced by Ian Anderson; engineered by Ian Anderson, Andrew Giddings and Leon Phillips.

Recording History: As related in Chapter 6, EMI came to Ian Anderson with the idea of doing an album of classical music for flute and orchestra. What ultimately occurred was that Anderson, in collaboration with Tull keyboard player Andy Giddings (billed as 'Andrew' on this more high-brow LP!), came up with an album of modern instrumental music with a lot of flute—the 'orchestra' was provided by Giddings' electronic keyboards. A few session musicians were brought in to fill out the sound with solos.

Comments: Divinities is one of the four or five best things Ian Anderson has ever done. Period. It's not Tull Music at all, but something more like very good film soundtrack music. Or modern classical music. Or New Age. Or World Music. Or something. Whatever label you want to put on it, it's bloody good. Every tune is complex and melodic, spiritually and emotionally felt and a tour de force for Anderson and his flute-playing abilities. Prior to the recording of the album Anderson had taken the time to relearn how to play the flute and this is the amazing result. The entire album is excellent but the highlights for me are 'In Sight Of The Minaret,' 'In The Grip Of Stronger Stuff' (which became a standard number performed by Jethro Tull in concert), 'At Their Father's Knee,' 'En Afrique,' 'In The Pay Of Spain' and 'In The Times Of India (Bombay Valentine).'

Trivia: On its first week of release, *Divinities* placed #1 on *Billboard*'s 'Top Classical Crossover' album chart. Anderson poked fun at this nonsensical category in concert by saying, 'The album hit number one on the Top Classical Crossover chart—whatever the fuck that is!'

Verdict: Brilliant. A must-have. 5/5

The Secret Language Of Birds

Released: March 2000
Track List: The Secret Language Of Birds; The Little Flower Girl; Montserrat; Postcard Day; The Water Carrier; Set-Aside; A Better Moon; Sanctuary; The Jasmine Corridor; The Habanero Reel; Panama Freighter; The Secret Language Of Birds, Part II; Boris Dancing; Circular Breathing; The Stormont Shuffle. Bonus tracks (live with Jethro Tull): In The Grip Of Stronger Stuff; Thick As A Brick. (All songs by Ian Anderson.)

Cover Art: Designed and illustrated by Bogdan Zarkowski, Zarkowski Designs. Another attractive and tasteful cover by Zarkowski, featuring a painting of two exotic birds perched in front of what appears to be a Rousseau-like rain forest with wide-eyed wild animals peeking out from behind the leaves.

Personnel: Ian Anderson (vocals, flute, acoustic guitar, bouzouki, acoustic bass guitar, mandolin, percussion, piccolo); Andrew Giddings (accordion, piano, organ, marimba, percussion, electric bass, keyboards and other orchestral sounds). With guests: Gerry Conway (drums on 2 tracks); Darren Mooney (drums on 2 tracks); James Duncan (drums on 1 track); Martin Barre (electric guitar on 2 tracks). Note: The 1998 line-up of Jethro Tull appears on the bonus tracks. Produced and engineered by Ian Anderson.

Recording History: The album was recorded at Ian Anderson's home studio during 1998. As mentioned in Chapter 6, the LP was completed and ready for release when Jethro Tull was signed to the new labels, Papillon and Fuel 2000. It was agreed that a proper Jethro Tull album be released first, so the new solo album was held back a year in deference to *J-Tull Dot Com*. Once again working with Andy Giddings, Anderson put together the LP with minimum input from other musicians.

Comments: The Secret Language Of Birds (or *SLOB*, as Anderson and fans affectionately call it) is the solo album everyone has expected from Ian Anderson since the 70s. It is mostly acoustic, with very little of what could be called 'rock.' The songs take on a catch-all 'World Music' label as Anderson explores themes influenced by his travels around the globe. Several are love songs, many have a melancholic ambience and others are humorous and clever. 'Boris Dancing' is a wild instrumental that is often played by Jethro Tull in concert and consists of tricky time signature changes (the 'Boris' in the title is Boris Yeltsin). As always, the musicianship is superb and even Anderson's battered voice is used to great advantage on this album; the tentative tonal qualities fit the themes and moods of the songs perfectly.

Verdict: A near-classic. Consistently rewarding. 4/5

Martin Barre Solo Albums

Martin Barre released a mail order CD and cassette entitled *A Summer Band* in 1993. It was sold through the Jethro Tull fanzine, *A New Day*. In 1994 he released his first official album and a follow-up in 1996.

A Trick Of Memory

Released: UK: May 1994; US: April 1994

Track List: Bug; Way Before Your Time; Bug Bee; Empty Café; Suspicion; I Be Thank You; A Blues For All Seasons; A Trick Of Memory; Steal; Another View; Cold Heart; Bug C; Morris Minus; In The Shade Of The Shadow. (All songs by Martin Barre.)

Cover Art: The cover is adorned with a sepia-tone photo of Martin Barre standing against a building. On the initial releases of the CD, the photo was cropped at Barre's waist and included the message 'Guitarist of Jethro Tull' beside his name. Barre objected and subsequent pressings feature the full-bodied photo without the Tull reference.

Personnel: Martin Barre (vocals, electric and acoustic guitars, flute, Hammond); Andy Giddings (keyboards); Marc Parnell (drums); Maggie Reeday (vocals); Matt Pegg (bass); Mel Collins (alto sax); Marc Johnstone (keyboards); Graham Ward (drums); Martin Allcock (double bass); Ric Sanders (violin); Rob Darnell (percussion); Nick Pentelow (sax); Richard Sidwell (trumpet); Steve Sidwell (trumpet); Tom Glendinning (drums); Mark Tucker (acoustic guitars, backing vocals, finger snaps); Gavyn Wright (violin); Wilf Gibson (violin); Tony Pleeth (cello); Garfield Jackson (viola); Malinda Maxwell (oboe); Joy Russell, Ian Frances, Katie Kissoon, Linda Taylor, Weston Foster (backing vocals). Produced by Martin Barre, co-production Mark Tucker.

Recording Background: Martin Barre gathered a group of musicians in the early 90s to perform at various clubs, fan conventions and outdoor events. Originally the group was called A Summer Band. A few former and current Jethro Tull members participated in the recording of this LP (Giddings, Allcock and swing-shift bass player Matt Pegg) during 1993.

Comments: It's not Jethro Tull. The music on *A Trick Of Memory* is quite different but that doesn't mean it's not any good. Barre has presented a group of eclectic vocal pop songs mixed with some *ripping* instrumentals that are more akin to something the Prog Rock group Camel might do. 'Jazz-rock fusion' could be a way to describe them. The vocal tunes are okay, some better than others, and Barre does a credible job singing. The title track, 'Suspicion,' 'Way Before Your Time' and 'Cold Heart' are memorable. There's nothing here that's going to make headlines but it's a solid, honest effort from a talented and often underrated musician.

Trivia: The LP was poorly distributed and is very rare.

Verdict: Very enjoyable. 3/5

The Meeting

Released: UK: March 1996; US: September 1996

Track List: The Meeting; The Potion; Outer Circle; I Know Your Face; Misere; Time After Time; Spanner; Running Free; Tom's; Dreamer; The Audition. (All songs by Martin Barre.)

Cover Art: Designed by Clive Hooper/Planographics. The cover depicts a simple, tasteful colour illustration of a cactus in the desert.

Personnel: Martin Barre (guitars, flute); Maggie Reeday (vocals); Jonathan Noyce (bass); Darren Mooney (drums); Andrew Murray (keyboards); Matt Pegg (bass); Gerry Conway (drums); Miles Bould (percussion); Mel Collins (sax); Doane Perry (drums); Mark Tucker (keyboards); Dave Mattacks (drums); Marc Parnell (drums); Paul Cox (vocals); Joy Russell (vocals); Ian Francis (backing vocals). Produced by Martin Barre, co-production by Mark Tucker.

Recording Background: Utilising the same methods and more or less the same personnel that contributed to his previous album, Martin Barre recorded the album at Presshouse Studios during 1995 and early 1996.

Comments: It could be called *A Trick Of Memory, Part II*, as it's a continuation of the same kind of music—good vocal pop songs and progressive rock instrumentals. The tracks 'Misere' and 'Spanner' have been performed by Jethro Tull in concert and are guitar showcases. 'I Know Your Face' sounds like it could be a Tull song because it features a flute riff that gets you bopping. Again, not a classic, but a worthwhile, fresh and solid LP.

Trivia: Only 1,000 copies of the Presshouse edition were made and sold through *A New Day*, making them collector's items.

Verdict: If you liked *A Trick Of Memory*, you'll like *The Meeting*! 3/5

Martin Barre also contributed to a limited release CD by his friend John Carter entitled *Spirit Flying Free* (credited to 'John Carter with Martin Barre'), released and distributed through *A New Day* in November 1996.

The Compilation Albums

Numerous Jethro Tull compilation and greatest hits albums have been released all over the world. This book attempts to briefly discuss the official UK and US releases. Any compilation that contained a significant amount of previously unreleased material is found in chapters 3 to 6.

M.U.—The Best Of Jethro Tull

Released: January 1976

Track List: Teacher (version #2); Aqualung (I. Anderson/J. Anderson); Thick As A Brick (edit #1); Bungle In The Jungle; Locomotive Breath; Fat Man; Living In The Past; A Passion Play (edit #8); Skating Away On The Thin Ice Of A New Day; Rainbow Blues; Nothing Is Easy. (All songs by Ian Anderson, except where indicated.)

Comments and Verdict: A pretty good single-LP compilation of the early years, although nothing from *This Was* is included. The song 'Rainbow Blues' is previously unreleased and is an out-take from the *WarChild* sessions. The version of 'Aqualung' is a different mix from the album version. (The 'M.U.' in the title stands for 'Musicians Union.') 4/5

Repeat—The Best Of Jethro Tull, Volume II

Released: UK: September 1977; US: November 1977

Track List: Minstrel In The Gallery; Cross-Eyed Mary; A New Day Yesterday; Bourée (J. S. Bach); Thick As A Brick (edit #4); WarChild; A Passion Play (edit #9); To Cry You A Song?; Too Old To Rock 'N' Roll—Too Young To Die; Glory Row. (All songs by Ian Anderson except where indicated.)

Comments and Verdict: More goodies from the early years. 'Glory Row' is an unreleased track, an out-take from the *WarChild* sessions. The single (edited) version of 'Minstrel In The Gallery' is included. 3/5

Original Masters

Released: UK: October 1985; US: November 1985

Track List: Living In The Past; Aqualung (I. Anderson/J. Anderson); Too Old To Rock 'N' Roll—Too Young To Die; Locomotive Breath; Skating Away On The Thin Ice Of A New Day; Bungle In The Jungle; Sweet Dream; Songs From The Wood; The Witch's Promise; Thick As A Brick (edit #1); Minstrel In The Gallery; Life Is A Long Song. (All songs by Ian Anderson except where indicated.)

Comments and Verdict: A much better compilation than the first two, but it's strange that for an album released in 1985, the latest song it has on it is 1977's 'Songs From The Wood'! 4/5

20 Years Of Jethro Tull

Released: UK: October 1988; US: January 1989

Track List: Stormy Monday Blues (Ecstine/Crowder/Hines); Love Story; A New Day Yesterday; Summerday Sands; March, The Mad Scientist; Lick Your Fingers Clean; Overhang; Crossword; Jack-A-Lynn; Part Of The Machine; Mayhem, Maybe; Kelpie; Wond'ring Aloud; Dun Ringill; Life Is A Long Song; Nursie; Grace; The Witch's Promise; Living In The Past; Aqualung (I. Anderson/J. Anderson); Locomotive Breath. (All songs by Ian Anderson except where indicated.)

Note: This track listing applies to the CD version. A double vinyl LP edition was also released that contained several more tracks.

Comments and Verdict: This is the single-CD 'abridged' version of the 3-CD box set entitled *20 Years Of Jethro Tull.* Suffice it to say that the box set is infinitely superior and I find the track selection on this truncated edition sorely lacking. Many of the better songs are missing. 3/5

The Best Of Jethro Tull—The Anniversary Collection

Released: UK: May 1993; US: June 1993

Track List: A Song For Jeffrey; Beggar's Farm (Anderson/Abrahams); A Christmas Song; A New Day Yesterday; Bourée (J. S. Bach);

Nothing Is Easy; Living In The Past; To Cry You A Song?; Teacher (version #2); Sweet Dream; Cross-Eyed Mary; Mother Goose; Aqualung (I. Anderson/J. Anderson); Locomotive Breath; Life Is A Long Song; Thick As A Brick (extract); A Passion Play (extract); Skating Away On The Thin Ice Of A New Day; Bungle In The Jungle; Minstrel In The Gallery; Too Old To Rock 'N' Roll—Too Young To Die; Songs From The Wood; Jack In The Green; The Whistler; Heavy Horses; Dun Ringill; Fylingdale Flyer; Jack-A-Lynn; Pussy Willow; Broadsword; Under Wraps #2; Steel Monkey; Farm On The Freeway; Jump Start; Kissing Willie; This Is Not Love. (All songs by Ian Anderson except where indicated.)

Comments and Verdict: I suppose if you're going to buy a Jethro Tull greatest hits collection, this is the one to get. A remastered, 2-disk set, it's got all of the 'hits' plus a few popular songs. My only complaint would be that it's short on material from the later years. 5/5

Through The Years

Released: UK: January 1997

Track List: Living In The Past (live); Wind-Up; WarChild; Dharma For One; Acres Wild; Budapest; The Whistler; We Used To Know; Beastie; Locomotive Breath (live); Rare And Precious Chain; Quizz Kid; Still Loving You Tonight. (All songs by Ian Anderson.)

Comments and Verdict: A UK-only release, the album contains a very odd potpourri of songs from all the various periods in Jethro Tull's history. I give it high marks simply for the unusual choices made in the selections. 4/5

The Very Best Of Jethro Tull

Released: July 2001

Track List: Living In The Past; Aqualung (I. Anderson/J. Anderson); Sweet Dream; The Whistler; Bungle In The Jungle; The Witch's Promise; Locomotive Breath; Steel Monkey; Thick As A Brick (extract); Bourée; Too Old To Rock 'N' Roll—Too Young To Die; Life Is A Long Song; Songs From The Wood; A New Day Yesterday; Heavy Horses; Broadsword; Roots To Branches; A Song For Jeffrey; Minstrel In The Gallery; Cheerio. (All songs by Ian Anderson except where indicated.)

Comments and Verdict: A long (over 70 minutes) remastered single-CD collection of obvious hits, but frankly, it's not long enough. What's here is certainly great but there is so much more! The versions of 'Heavy Horses' and 'Minstrel In The Gallery' included here are also edited, which is a bummer. 4/5

UK EPs and Singles
(Excluding Promo Or Cancelled Releases)

'Sunshine Day'/'Aeroplane' February 1968

'A Song For Jeffrey'/'One For John Gee' September 1968

'Love Story'/'A Christmas Song' November 1968

'Living In The Past'/'Driving Song' May 1969

'Sweet Dream'/'17' October 1969

'The Witch's Promise'/'Teacher' (version #1) January 1970

'Inside'/'Alive And Well And Living In' May 1970

(EP) 'Life Is A Long Song'/'Up The Pool'/'Dr Bogenbroom'/'From Later'/ 'Nursie' September 1971

'Bungle In The Jungle'/'Back-Door Angels' November 1974

'Minstrel In The Gallery'/'Summerday Sands' August 1975

'Living In The Past'/'Requiem' January 1976

'Too Old To Rock 'N' Roll—Too Young To Die'/'Rainbow Blues' March 1976

(EP) 'Ring Out, Solstice Bells'/'March, The Mad Scientist'/'A Christmas Song'/'Pan Dance' December 1976

'The Whistler'/'Strip Cartoon' February 1977

'Moths'/'Life Is A Long Song' April 1978

'A Stitch In Time'/'Sweet Dream' (live) September 1978

'North Sea Oil'/'Elegy' October 1979

(EP) 'Home'/'King Henry's Madrigal'/'Warm Sporran'/'Ring Out, Solstice Bells' November 1979

'Working John, Working Joe'/'Fylingdale Flyer' October 1980

'Broadsword'/'Fallen On Hard Times' May 1982

'Lap Of Luxury'/'Astronomy'/'Automotive Engineering'/'Tundra' September 1984

'Coronach'/'Jack Frost And The Hooded Crow' June 1986

'Steel Monkey'/'Down At The End Of Your Road' October 1987

(EP) 'Steel Monkey'/'Down At The End Of Your Road'/'Too Many Too'/ 'I'm Your Gun' October 1987

'Said She Was A Dancer'/'Dogs In The Midwinter' January 1988

(EP) 'Said She Was A Dancer'/'Dogs In The Midwinter'/'The Waking Edge' January 1988

(EP) 'Part Of The Machine'/'Stormy Monday Blues'/'Lick Your Fingers Clean'/'Minstrel In The Gallery'/'Farm On The Freeway' June 1988

'Another Christmas Song'/'A Christmas Song' (live) December 1989

(EP) 'Another Christmas Song'/'A Christmas Song' (live)/'Cheap Day Return' (live)/'Mother Goose' (live)/'Locomotive Breath' (live) December 1989

'This Is Not Love'/'Night In The Wilderness' August 1991

(EP) 'This Is Not Love'/'Night In The Wilderness'/'Jump Start' (live) August 1991

(EP) 'Rocks On The Road'/'Jack-A-Lynn' (demo)/'Like A Tall Thin Girl' (live)/'Fat Man' (live) (CD1) March 1992

(EP) 'Rocks On The Road' (live)/'Bourée' (live)/'Mother Goose' (live); 'Jack-A-Lynn' (live)/'Aqualung/Locomotive Breath' (live) (CD2) March 1992

'Rocks On The Road'/'Jack-A-Lynn' (demo) March 1992

'Rocks On The Road' (12' remix)/'Jack-A-Lynn' (demo)/'Aqualung/Locomotive Breath' (live) March 1992

'Living In The Past'/'Hardliner' May 1993

'Living In The Past' (12' club remix)/'Living In The Past'/'Living In The Past' (Ravey Master Mix)/'Living In The Past' (NY Tip Mix) May 1993

(EP) 'Living In The (Slightly More Recent) Past'/'Silver River Turning'/'Rosa On The Factory Floor'/'I Don't Want To Be Me' (CD1) May 1993

(EP) 'Living In The Past'/'Truck Stop Runner'/'Piece Of Cake'/'Man Of Principle' (CD2) May 1993

(EP) 'Bends Like A Willow'/'Dot Com' (edit)/'It All Trickles Down' November 1999

US Singles
(Excluding Promo Or Cancelled Releases)

'Love Story'/'A Song For Jeffrey' February 1969

'Living In The Past'/'Driving Song' July 1969

'Sweet Dream'/'Back To The Family' November 1969

'The Witch's Promise'/'Teacher' (version #2) January 1970

'Inside'/'A Time For Everything' June 1970

'Hymn 43'/'Mother Goose' June 1971

'Locomotive Breath'/'Wind-Up' November 1971

'Living In The Past'/'A Christmas Song' October 1972

'A Passion Play (edit #8)'/'A Passion Play (edit #9)' April 1973
'A Passion Play (edit #10)'/'A Passion Play (edit #6)' September 1973
'Living In The Past'/'Cross-Eyed Mary' January 1974
'Bungle In The Jungle'/'Back-Door Angels' September 1974
'Skating Away'/'Sea Lion' February 1975
'Minstrel In The Gallery'/'Summerday Sands' August 1975
'Locomotive Breath'/'Fat Man' January 1976
'Too Old To Rock 'N' Roll—Too Young To Die'/'Bad-Eyed And Love-less' June 1976
'The Whistler'/'Strip Cartoon' March 1977
'Home'/'Warm Sporran' October 1979
'Fallen On Hard Times'/'Pussy Willow' June 1982
'Steel Monkey'/'Down At The End Of Your Road' October 1987
'Kissing Willie'/'Ears Of Tin' October 1989 (cassette single)
(EP) 'Rocks On The Road'/'Rocks On The Road' (live)/'Bourée' (live)/ 'Jack-A-Lynn' (demo)/'Night In The Wilderness'/'Jump Start' (live) April 1992 (CD5)
'A Christmas Song'/'Skating Away' November 1994

Videos/DVDs

Slipstream: *Released:* UK: August 1981; US: February 1983. *Comments:* Much of this video is a filmed concert from 1980 at the Hammersmith Odeon, featuring the *"A"* tour and line-up (Anderson, Barre, Pegg, Jobson, Craney). Additional studio footage includes a music video of 'Too Old To Rock 'N' Roll—Too Young To Die.' 3/5

20 Years Of Jethro Tull: *Released:* UK: October 1988; US: September 1989. *Comments:* Uneven documentary celebrating the 20th anniversary of Jethro Tull. At times there are disconcerting jumps in chronology. Highlights, however, include footage from the live satellite concert from Madison Square Garden in 1978 and music videos from *Under Wraps* and *Crest Of A Knave*. 3/5

25th Anniversary Video: *Released:* UK: July 1994; US: October 1994. *Comments:* A much better documentary celebrating the 25th anniversary of Jethro Tull. More interesting archival clips are included. A 30-minute bonus section features complete archival clips from various television appearances, 'The Story Of The Hare Who Lost His Spectacles' concert film and live performance footage. 4/5

Living With The Past (DVD): *Released:* May 2002. *Comments:* Jethro Tull's first music-DVD is a pleasure and nicely complements the live CD of the same title. Produced in conjunction with Classic Rock Productions, the bulk of the DVD is a live concert at London's Hammersmith Apollo Theatre on 25 November, 2001. Additional material is drawn from various other venues on the same tour. Numbers by the original 1968 line-up, captured live in a small club in England, are interspersed, as well as two acoustic tracks performed with a string quartet. Bonus material include numbers by Fairport Convention and Uriah Heep (both featuring Ian Anderson on guest flute and/or vocals), a photo gallery, a brief selection of bloopers and comments from fans and band members. Ian Anderson provides a public service announcement to promote awareness of DVT (deep vein thrombosis) from which he almost died in 1996 and there is an extract of a song shot from three different spots in the theatre (the viewer can choose from which seat to watch the performance). The DVD has a problem in that interview snippets are cut in between songs and sometimes over the music itself. For example, Jonathan Noyce is heard talking about the bass solo in 'Bourée' *during* the bass solo. Personally, I dislike concert films that splice interviews into the music and I realise that this is done often. I feel it's a jarring practice that distracts from the mood established by the concert. After all, how often does one get to see and hear Jethro Tull live from a multitude of camera angles, up close and personal? The interview clips are fine and interesting, but they tend to become tedious after one or two viewings. Give me the concert as is and put all the interviews in a bonus section! That said, the DVD looks great, sounds reasonably good (the volume of the concert footage is lower than that of the interviews) and it captures Tull in a top-notch performance. The 1968 band reunion tracks are remarkably tight, as if the guys had been playing together all this time. The two acoustic numbers with the string quartet are worth the price of the disc. Even though the DVD is lacking on the expected archival material, it is a fan's delight.

4/5

References

The Author's Top 10 Favourite Albums

Thick As A Brick (1972)
Aqualung (1971)
Songs From The Wood (1977)
Stand Up (1969)
Roots To Branches (1995)
Living In The Past (1972)
20 Years Of Jethro Tull (box set) (1988)
A Passion Play (1973)
Heavy Horses (1978)
Minstrel In The Gallery (1975)

Bibliography

Espinoza, Barbara. *Driving In Diverse: A Collective Profile Of Jethro Tull*. Morris Publishing (Nebraska), 1999.

Nollen, Scott Allen. *Jethro Tull—A History Of The Band, 1968-2001*. McFarland & Company, Inc. (North Carolina), 2001.

Rees, David. *Minstrel In The Gallery—A History Of Jethro Tull*. Firefly Publishing (UK), 1998.

Rees, David, ed. *A New Day* (Magazine). David Rees, Publisher (UK).

Russo, Greg. *Flying Colours: The Jethro Tull Reference Manual*. Crossfire Publications (New York), 2000.

Schramm, Karl and Gerard J. Burns, eds. *Jethro Tull, 25th: Complete Lyrics*. Palmyra Publishers (Germany), 1993.

Tull Publications, Fan Clubs, Internet Sites

Official Jethro Tull Website. www.j-tull.com - The best site, naturally. Contains bios of all the band members, discography, news updates, tour information and periodic messages from Ian Anderson.

A New Day magazine. Contact DavidRees1@compuserve.com, 75 Wren Way, Farnborough, Hants. GU14 8TA UK. Excellent fanzine published regularly (but not on a specific schedule) since 1985. Also check out A New Day Records website at www.anewdayrecords.co.uk

Beggar's Farm. German Jethro Tull fan club c/o Harald Eikermann, Sonnenallee 118, 12045 Berlin, Germany.

Itullians. Italian fan club: www.itullians.freeweb.supereva.it - Contact Aldo Tagliaferro ataglia@hotmail.com

Living In The Past magazine. Contact Dennis Landau wingedisle@aol.com, P.O. Box 1127, New Hyde Park, N.Y.11040, USA. Not as in-depth as *A New Day* but still worthwhile.

This Is Not The Way Ian Planned It! Jethro Tull info-magazine. Contact Bert Maessen, Rijksweg Noord 270, Sittard 6136 AG, The Netherlands.

Cup Of Wonder website. www.cupofwonder.com/tulllink.html - A fan-operated website. Lots of info, trivia and cool stuff.

Jethro Tull Webring. www.ringsurf.com/netring?ring=tullring;action=list - A catch-all listing of various Tull-related websites.

The Essential Library: Currently Available

Film Directors:

Woody Allen (2nd)	Tim Burton	Ang Lee
Jane Campion*	John Carpenter	Joel & Ethan Coen (2nd)
Jackie Chan	Steve Soderbergh	Clint Eastwood
David Cronenberg	Terry Gilliam*	Michael Mann
Alfred Hitchcock (2nd)	Krzysztof Kieslowski*	Roman Polanski
Stanley Kubrick (2nd)	Sergio Leone	Oliver Stone
David Lynch	Brian De Palma*	George Lucas
Sam Peckinpah*	Ridley Scott (2nd)	James Cameron
Orson Welles (2nd)	Billy Wilder	
Steven Spielberg	Mike Hodges	

Film Genres:

Blaxploitation Films	Bollywood	French New Wave
Horror Films	Spaghetti Westerns	Vietnam War Movies
Slasher Movies	Film Noir	German Expresionist Films
Vampire Films*	Heroic Bloodshed*	

Film Subjects:

Laurel & Hardy	Marx Brothers	Film Music
Steve McQueen*	Marilyn Monroe	The Oscars® (2nd)
Filming On A Microbudget	Bruce Lee	Writing A Screenplay
Film Studies		

TV:

Doctor Who

Literature:

Cyberpunk	Philip K Dick	The Beat Generation
Agatha Christie	Sherlock Holmes	Noir Fiction*
Terry Pratchett	Hitchhiker's Guide (2nd)	Alan Moore
William Shakespeare		

Ideas:

Conspiracy Theories	Nietzsche	UFOs
Feminism	Freud & Psychoanalysis	Bisexuality

History:

Alchemy & Alchemists	The Crusades	The Black Death
Jack The Ripper	The Rise Of New Labour	Ancient Greece
American Civil War	American Indian Wars	

Miscellaneous:

The Madchester Scene	Stock Market Essentials	Jethro Tull
How To Succeed As A Sports Agent		
How To Succeed In The Music Business		

Available at all good bookstores or send a cheque (payable to 'Oldcastle Books') to: **Pocket Essentials (Dept JT), 18 Coleswood Rd, Harpenden, Herts, AL5 1EQ, UK.** £3.99 each (£2.99 if marked with an *). For each book add 50p postage & packing in the UK and £1 elsewhere.